"There is no way to peace. Peace is the way."

— A.J. Muste

Bottom Dog Press

Come Together
Imagine Peace

Edited by Philip Metres,
Ann Smith & Larry Smith
Introduction by Philip Metres

Harmony Series
Bottom Dog Press
Huron, Ohio

Bottom Dog Press
PO Box 425/ Huron, 44839
http://members.aol.com/Lsmithdog/bottomdog
ISBN 978-1-933964-22-5

Credits:
Cover art: "Steps to Peace"
book logo "Peace Symbol Calligraphy"
from Desert Rose Press
Cover Layout and Design:
Kristen Schoewe
Book Layout: Larry Smith

Acknowledgments
Images by <desertrosepress.com>
Also see: <www.raventalk.com>

For a full list of credits and acknowledgments
see page 203.

We thank John Carroll University and
the Ohio Arts Council
for continued support.

Ohio Arts Council
A STATE AGENCY
THAT SUPPORTS PUBLIC
PROGRAMS IN THE ARTS

Table of Contents

Section Three: Call and Answer:
Poems of Exhortation & Action

Section Four: Healing the Breach:
Poems of Reconciliation

Section Five: Savoring the World:
Poems of Shared Humanity

Section Six: The Way We Learn to Love the World: Poems of Wildness & Home

Section Seven: Becoming the Next Thread: Poems of Ritual & Vigil

Section Eight: Gentleness that Wears Away Rock: Poems of Meditation & Prayer

Two Prefaces by Larry and Ann Smith

One

"Poetry is a weapon loaded with future." Gabriel Zelaya

This line by Zelaya transforms a military metaphor into one of resistance and hope. And this has been the guiding intention of this gathering of voices to image a world where peace is possible. And the solicited poems did come pouring in from all parts of the country and the world. We editors here at Bottom Dog Press have been beautifully rewarded by having these poems speak to us and our world. The volume challenged us, and the best works collected here offer truth and beauty, confrontation, resistance, and hope, each in their own way. As Gary Snyder's poem "For the Children" indicates, we all must do this peace work to preserve this world. And so in a larger sense these poems are for us all. To lead us off of the newspaper and into the compassion and understanding that alone can sustain us as people of the world.

Ann and I have been fortunate to have the critic and poet Philip Metres join us on this project. His introduction here and his detailed study *Behind the Lines: War Resistance Poetry on the American Homefront Since 1941* (University of Iowa 2007) collect and extend the work of the many poets who would move us toward a peaceable world.

I love the "Precedent" poems included here, for they remind us that our work includes history and models which we can learn from and adapt to our own times. These writers all take us back through Walt Whitman to Emerson's definition of the poet's role: "The poet is the sayer, the namer, and represents beauty," and so a truthful "naming" and "saying" are a part of all of these beautiful poems. The poets here have made statements on peace and poetry that guide and inspire.

Denise Levertov's poem "Life at War," written during the Vietnam War, speaks to us immediately and directly by naming what has been lost in adopting a contemporary mindset of continuous warfare: "our nerve filaments twitch in its presence/ day and night,/ nothing we say has not the husky phlegm of it in the saying,/ nothing we do has the quickness, the sureness,/ the deep intelligence living at peace would have." For her and the poets and readers here the poem bravely confronts the world and yet moves us to imagine the peace within it and ourselves. We offer this book as part of that intention.

— Larry Smith (October 2008)

Two

In developing the idea for this book, we wanted to create a place for people to go who needed a vision of the world that could balance the anxiety, fear, and conflict that are being sent out over airwaves in the guise of News and the Truth. This is a collection of poetry meant to help us to Imagine Peace. As I read the poems that poured in, I was moved by the number of people thinking and writing about "peace." In my mind peace is an abstract phenomenon that ranges from very basic and simple to overwhelmingly complex. So, when I read the diverse interpretations and images from these authors, I realized that it takes a book like this with its richness and variety to help us to articulate, define and live peace.

The poems in this book include descriptions of the destruction humans can bring upon ourselves and others. It also includes acts of humanity and compassion that can emerge like the dandelion that grows in the crack of a sidewalk. From my perspective of the world, in which I have not experienced a war but have witnessed the suffering of others, I relate especially to the poems of awakening and unseen heroism. Maj Ragain's "Willows" expresses the ways everyone, including young children, is affected by the atmosphere of war and the loss of innocence. Wislawa Szymborska uses simple language to capture the pain and healing of cleaning up the aftermath of war in "The End and the Beginning." From classical and historical poems to contemporary, these poets use language to paint us pictures with all the color and richness of a painter's palette. We hope you enjoy all of them and savor the ones that speak directly to you.

— Ann Smith (October 2008)

Ann and I dedicate our work on this book to
two Peacemakers:
Jean Goldfarb and Bill Wright

Introduction to *Come Together: Imagine Peace*

"*Peace* poetry?!" a friend snorted, when I told him about this anthology of peace poetry. "I mean, *what is that,* anyway?"

A poet himself, my friend's allegiance is to language, to poetry's fundamental independence. Almost everything we have been taught about literature seems to militate against the notion of "peace poetry": great stories have conflict at their core; characters are born in and borne by the winds of potentially destructive desires; out of the quarrel with ourselves comes poetry; great poetry resists programmatic politics and the totalizing claims of ideology; *ad infinitum.*

Western literature begins with the rage of Achilles and the long siege of Troy, and scatters corpses with as much intensity and gore as a 21st century action thriller. In Homer's heroic epic poem *The Iliad,* only Thersites—a minor figure—momentarily gives voice to all those who hate war, and is battered back into silence. The poem ends ominously, at the brink of the rape and pillage of Troy, whose muted civilians tremble in the background. *The Iliad* instigates but never resolves the great dilemma of war poetry: How to write poetry in times of conflict that does not, in the process, end up glorifying and perpetuating war?

Let's face it. Everyone believes Dante's *Inferno* is far more intriguing than his *Paradiso.* We relish the drama in conflict, failure, suffering. Heaven is boring, inhuman even. But would we really want to live in hell?

Fast-forward to the 20th century. In his Imagist Manifesto (published as "A Few Don'ts for an Imagiste" in *Poetry* in 1913), Ezra Pound exhorted poets toward a poetics of the particular, away from fuzzy abstractions—a poetic orientation that has dominated modern poetry. He warned: "Don't use such an expression as 'dim lands of *peace.*' It dulls the image. It mixes an abstraction with the concrete. It comes from the writer's not realizing that the natural object is always the *adequate* symbol." Pound's "dim lands of *peace*" is no coincidence, written in the years before the so-called "War To End All Wars"; it underscores doubly the trouble for poets invested in imagining peace. Despite the modern revulsion to war—voiced most plangently by Wilfred Owen, and most acidly by Siegfried Sassoon during World War I—our language all too often has participated in or been complicit with conflict, domination, and mass violence.

Even if modern poetry is predominantly anti-war, the great work of poetic dissent too often has articulated itself as resistance to the dominant narrative, rather than offering another way. How to imagine peace, how to make peace? Even poet Denise Levertov found herself at a loss for words at a panel in the 1980s, when confronted by psychologist Virginia Satir, who said that "poets should present to the world images of peace, not only of war; everyone needed to be able to imagine peace if we were going to achieve it." In her response, an essay called "Poetry and Peace: Some Broader Dimensions" (1989), Levertov argues that "peace as a positive condition of society, not merely as an interim between wars, is something so unknown that it casts no images on the mind's screen." There is something about the very word "peace" that resists static images, or tends toward the cliché (the dove, the two-fingered V, the peace sign, etc.).

Our lexicon for peacemaking is poor, not because we have no experience of peace or peacemaking, but because the language of violence and war has been ubiquitous in our culture, and enormously profitable for those in power. And with the mightiest military in the history of the world, in perhaps the most adaptable empire, we live under conditions that Paul Virilio, borrowing from William James, calls *Pure War*—a state in which the endless preparation for war constitutes the real war.

If "peace" seems abstract, foggy, weak, and utopian, is this a problem of language or the poverty of our culture? The word *peace* has rich etymological roots, from the Latin *pacem*, and related to the Greek *eirene*, which was used by translators to evoke the Hebrew word "shalom," meaning peace, welfare, and prosperity. *Pax* meant a "treaty of peace, tranquility, absence of war," and peace appeared in the 12th century in Anglo-Norman as "freedom from civil disorder," was related to the word "fasten," and replaced the Old English term which also meant "happiness." The notion of "peace of mind" dates from the 13th century. Peace then is not merely the absence of war or conflict, but the presence of positive social, ecological, and spiritual relations. To these definitions, we should add Gandhi's notion of *satyagraha* (truth force) or what Levertov calls in her poem "Making Peace"—"an energy field more intense than war." To use A.J. Muste's phrase, itself echoing Buddhist and Taoist teachings: "There is no way to peace. Peace is the way."

What would a poetry of peace look like? As Levertov wrote in "Poetry and Peace," "if a poetry of peace is ever to be written, there must first be this stage we are just entering—the poetry of preparation for peace, a poetry of protest, of lament, of praise for the living earth; a poetry that demands justice, renounces violence, reveres mystery." Poetry, and its modern lyric embodiment in song, has been an ideal partner for the peace movement's homespun, community-building efforts, solidifying the commitment of the already-converted and hailing the uncertain populace. Muriel Rukeyser, who hearkens back to the original meaning of poetry as *poeisis*, a making, writes, "I will protest all my life….but I'm a person who makes…and I have decided that whenever I protest…I will make something—I will make poems, plant, feed children, build, but not ever protest without making something."

More than mere protest, the poems of *Come Together: Imagine Peace* demonstrate the range that Levertov anticipates: elegiac, hortatory, ecological, and spiritual poems from the complex to the simple, the conflictual to the harmonious, the lyric to the narrative, the baggy to the supple, the hectoring to the longing, the melancholic to the ecstatic, the provocative to the meditative. They demonstrate that peace is more like a house than a dream. They are not naively utopian, and, like John Milton in "Aereopagitica," argue against "a fugitive and cloistered virtue, unexercised and unbreathed, that never sallies out and sees her adversary." In his words, if "that which purifies us is trial, and trial is by what is contrary," then a vital poetry of peace necessarily must confront its own blind spots, its own misplaced goodwill, its own utopian flights. According to scholar Michael True, "although writings in [the nonviolent tradition] resemble conventional proclamations recommending peace reform, their tone and attitude tend to be provocative, even disputatious, rather than conciliatory" (xi).

To the great traditions of war poetry and antiwar poetry, represented in such anthologies as *A Poetry Reading Against the Vietnam War* (eds. Robert Bly and David Ray, 1967), *Against Forgetting: Twentieth Century Poetry of Witness* (ed. Carolyn Forché, 1991), and *Poets Against the War* (ed. Sam Hamill, 2003), *Come Together: Imagine Peace* brings the dead and the living, poetic luminaries, prophetic firebrands, and quieter, more common voices into a chorus for peace.

Section One. Some Precedents.

The poetry of peace already exists in the footnotes and margins of political and literary history, originating in the earliest writings in ancient Sumer, such as Enheduanna's "Lament to the Spirit of War," and felt acutely in the anti-Homeric love poetry of Sappho, who begins our anthology. It is a poetry that is not quite a tradition. Rather, it is a tendency, an itch or irritation, a dormant virus that we've carried with us, a longing like thirst, a half-caught dream, within poetry's longstanding and rocky courtship with power. The poetry of peace is a writing against the grain of received narratives and histories, against the notion that we are doomed to violence and war.

The poetry, or rather, poetries, of peace—part of the dissident root system of all national poetries—themselves are diverse, extending like rhizomes in multiple directions. *Come Together: Imagine Peace* begins with a selection of Precedents, the prophetic voices that lay claim to other ways of being. The Precedents anticipate and invite the various contemporary visions of peace from the rest of the book. Though this anthology has no pretense to being a comprehensive historical and multinational archive of peace poems— which could also include, just from the Anglo-American tradition, a host of poems, from John Milton's "Nativity Ode" to T.S. Eliot's "The Waste Land," with its concluding longing for "shantih shantih shantih" ("the peace which passeth all understanding"). Yet it proposes that peace poetry—like the peace movement that it anticipates, reflects, and argues with—is part of a larger human conversation about the possibility of a more just and pacific system of social and ecological relations.

While Sappho couples poetry with erotic desire, Walt Whitman's minor poem, "As I Ponder'd in Silence," stands as an epigraph to his great poetic vision of human unity in "Song of Myself" and the Civil War poems, and his struggle to claim the sacredness of the human body as the center of a modern poetry and modern spirituality. Other poems, such as Emily Dickinson's #739 and Robert Creeley's "For No Clear Reason," vividly demonstrate the longing for an end to psychic turbulence that has marked the great religious writing from the teachings of Buddha to St. Augustine's *Confessions* ("our hearts are restless until they rest in You").

In contrast, a number of Precedents cast their unswerving eye upon the ruins of war. C. P. Cavafy's "Waiting for the Barbarians," Kenneth Rexroth's "August 22, 1939," Robert Lowell's "Fall 1961," and June Jordan's "The Bombing of Baghdad," witness to and perform elegies for the cultural, political, ecological, physical, and emotional devastations that come with war— how it robs us of our most basic ability to name ourselves (except in opposition to some barbarian other), to care for our children ("a father's no shield for his child"), and to claim our common humanity.

Yet, like more recent peace poetry, this genealogy of Precedents anchors itself in the vital vision embodied by resisters, demonstrators, peacemakers, and prophets. Edna St. Vincent Millay's "Conscientious Objector," Karl Shapiro's "The Conscientious Objector," William Stafford's "Peace Walk," and Denise Levertov's "The Altars in the Street" offer compelling visions of peace action, which become touchstones for contemporary poets' attempts to narrate what gets left out of the daily news. Relatedly, Kenneth Patchen's "Creation," Muriel Rukeyser's "Poem," William Stafford's "At the Un-National Monument Along the Canadian Border," and Denise Levertov's "Making Peace," theorize what peacework might look like, and how it might be sustained.

Finally, Allen Ginsberg's visionary "Wichita Vortex Sutra"—from which we have excerpted the moment in which the poet incants a declaration of the end of the Vietnam War—asserts the performative power of language, language as prayer, like Audre Lorde's "A Litany for Survival," Yehuda Amichai's "Wildpeace," and Mahmoud Darwish's concluding litany of salaams from "State of Siege." These poems establish the difficulties of overcoming our own distrust, borne out of histories of oppression, in finding a way toward resolving conflict and reconciliation with each other, and with ourselves.

Section Two. The Story So Far: Poems of Witness & Elegy

The great war poems confront war with frank honesty, sometimes bitter anger, and great compassion for war's victims. In homage to that tradition, and in line with the work of Carolyn Forché in *Against Forgetting: Twentieth Century Poetry of Witness*, the poems in "The Story So Far" face history and its brutal tides. Though human history often has been framed as a history of wars, these poems mark both the human capacity for violence and its selective memory. From Wislawa Szymborska's sympathetic ant-eye view of the battlefield, where unphotographed "someones" must clean up the rubble, to Joseph Ross' ominously titled "On a Sign Announcing: *Expanding Arlington National Cemetery*," from John Bradley's austere image of two dead lovers (one Muslim, one Serb) on a bridge between Bosnian and Serbian neighborhoods in Sarajevo to Carolyn Forché's stark recognition that "the heart is the toughest part of the body," these poems grieve, rage, and count the dead, catalyzing our weariness into a state of watchful vigil.

Section Three. Call and Answer: Poems of Exhortation & Action

The poems in "Call and Answer" are not mere protest poems, but rather a dialectic between exhortations and actions—in essence, calls to action and representations of action. Demonstrative and demonstrational, these poems offer rousing rhetorics and language templates for social change. Poems by Robert Bly and Lawrence Ferlinghetti urge us to speak out, to defy the conventions of polite non-political speech in both poetry and in the public sphere, to "become worthy of our dead." These poems offer vivid models of dissent and resistance that burn in the memory: William Heyen's "black bows and ribbons," Liane Ellison Norman's image of seven-year-old Maya Weiss's anti-war rally, Edward Dougherty's saffron-robed monks beating drums, Martín Espada's song for Iraq War C.O. Sgt. Mejía, among others. Still other poems complicate the notions of patriotism and the peace movement. Adrienne Rich's meditation on patriotism ("a patriot is not a weapon") is as unsparing about those in the peace movement who failed to be roused equally for the struggles for justice. Equally essential is Robert Pinsky's acerbic questioning of "peace" as a quietism that fails to acknowledge our fully complex and animal humanity.

Section Four. Healing the Breach: Poems of Reconciliation

While peace poetry may occasionally provoke, it also must dramatize the sometimes tentative, sometimes outlandish reaching across the abyssal distances between antagonists. In "Healing the Breach," the poems bring to life stunning acts of reconciliation and peacemaking from the past and present, between nations and individuals. The vision of French and German soldiers playing soccer on the Christmas Eve truce during World War I, captured magically by Robert Cording; Naomi Shihab Nye's visionary conclusion to "Jerusalem"—"it's late, but everything happens next"; Aharon Shabtai's provocative offering of his daughter to his nation's "enemy"; Naton Leslie's act of forgiveness of an abusive father; these poems articulate the various "points we meet," as Elmaz Abinader's poem puts it, and show both courage and consanguinity in their trust that such acts of reaching will not be in vain.

Section Five. Savoring the World: Poems of Shared Humanity

Though *Come Together: Imagine Peace* is not quite a global anthology, much peace poetry shows it globalist leanings in its vision of common humanity. Descendents of Whitman, these poets in "Savoring the World" imagine and assert the persistence of our connectedness, so obscured by ideologies, languages, and national security walls. Taking us from the road to Rama (and its South Asian narrative of journey), we stop in Palestine, Lebanon, Washington D.C., Darfur, Hanoi, El Salvador, the Dixwell Stop and Shop, the equator, Manhattan, the Pennsylvania State Correctional Institute for Men at Houtzdale, outside Salaam's in Pittsburgh, to some unnamed street where a woman's "mind is at war." In Anna Meek's words, "we cannot steal ourselves from one another." These poems pronounce that humanity does not end at the national border, nor, increasingly, do we, global citizens and descendents from elsewheres.

Section Six. The Way We Learn to Love the World: Poems of Wildness & Home

If "Nature holds up a mirror"—a line that Robert Lowell, in "Fall 1961," derives from Shakespeare—we have often sought ourselves and the beyond of ourselves in *wildness*. During World War II, William Stafford recounted how conscientious objectors working in alternative service camps in the wilds of the United States often sought to become "the quiet of the land." In "The Way We Learn to Love the World," the poems look to the natural world and to the home for images of hope, so vividly begun by Wendell Berry in "The Peace of Wild Things." Though we see in nature the fear and violence that is also in us, in Todd Davis' "Trying to Understand the Patriot Act," we also see where such fear emerges, and how we might quiet it. "Stillness is a choice you make," as Emily Bright's poem attests. Alongside the poems of wildness, the poems that mark the boundaries of home suggest the vulnerabilities and possibilities cradled in our dwelling places; in the presence of the hardiness of dandelions, in the evanescence of fireflies, in "tires in the rain," these poems "report," as Jeff Gundy's title puts it, "on the Conditions in the Interior."

Section Seven. Becoming the Next Thread: Poems of Rituals & Vigils

To order the anarchies inside and outside us, the poems of ritual and vigil offer word structures that parallel the practices of allowing the sacred to happen. To find ways to structure our days, to find rhythm where demand so often imposes, these poems dramatize and become rituals and vigils in themselves. From Angie Estes' recipes to Judith Montgomery's weaving, these poems take tactile acts and sound as literal and metaphorical ways of "becoming the next thread." Here, we find Yusef Komunyakaa's arresting, grief-heavy "Facing It," where the speaker seems half-disappeared in the Vietnam Veteran Memorial wall; his unstinting grief makes him a figure of anamnesis. It is not surprising, either, to find three sonnets (Robert Cording's "Opening Cans," Dave Lucas' "The Fourteen Happy Days," and Katharyn Howd Machan's "At the Veterans Hospital") in this section, as if that structuring form—with its argument, turn, and resolution—could become the objective correlative of peace ritual itself.

Section Eight. Gentleness that Wears Away Rock: Poems of Meditation & Prayer

Taken from a line by Ellen Bass's "Pray for Peace," this section of poems weaves together prayers, blessings, kwansabas, and glyphs into a chorus like the gentle constancy of water that "wears away rock." Poems of meditation and prayer merge physical being with spiritual being. No wonder, then, that poems such as "Zazen" by Jennifer Karmin and "Wind" by Ahimsa Timoteo Bodrán bring contemplative mindfulness and attention to breathing, that oscillation between our taking in the world and letting it go. Ranging from catalogues of everyday being, to musings on the nature of God (Fady Joudah's "Proposal"), to songs for the nationalities of the former Yugoslavia (Karen Kovacik's "Songs for a Belgrade Baker"), to prayers by Jesuit peace activist Daniel Berrigan, these poems demonstrate the range of mindfulness and calling forth to higher powers, both within and without us. They often assert a disarming earnestness, a faith in the goodness of things that is leavened by nimbleness of mind, leaps of compassion, and occasionally acid wit.

Come Together: Imagine Peace

There may yet come a time when this poetry can be called a tradition, if even a minor tradition. This anthology is an attempt to draw back to in order to move forward, the way a rower leans forward into the water and then digs backward, in order to propel into some new territory. At the very least, *Come Together: Imagine Peace* introduces the poets to each other, often doing parallel work without the benefit of mutual support (see the bio pages for more information). Equally important, *Come Together* offers a bridge between our poetry communities and peace communities, those places where we find ourselves.

Poet and Vietnam Veteran W.D. Ehrhart recently mused:

> What was the point of my reading antiwar poetry to the members of the Brandywine Peace Community? These are folks who chain themselves to fences and hammer on missile warheads. But what they hear in my poems confirms them in their beliefs (which are not easy to hold and maintain in this culture)…and renews their spirit and commitment; it gives them a sense of connectedness, of not being entirely alone. That's worth doing, even if it is on such a small scale (there were maybe 25 people there that night).

We hope that these poets and poems will be seen not only as food for the peace troops in moments of repose, but also as a script for future readings, demonstrations and other actions. Peace poems, after all, are often occasional endeavors, written by movement participants and delivered for the ear and heart. Gene Sharp's *Politics of Nonviolent Action* lists 198 nonviolent tactics that resisters have employed to resist illegitimate power and effect social change. Poems can take their place as part of the peace movement story and community building that is so central to peace movement labor. These poems invite us to join the local networks of the peace movement—which, lacking serious mass media attention and much of the nation, always needs more active participants—those who can bring a dish to a potluck discussion on the war in Iraq, those who can post flyers or canvass one's neighborhood, those who can write press releases and speeches. Poets have a pivotal role to play in the peace movement, because of our keen attention to language—not simply to excoriate its abuse by the dominant narrative, but also to construct alternative narratives that invite those who may be sympathetic but lack awareness of the movement, to learn, join and act.

We look forward to poets who might become creators as well as archivists of this movement, who might become mediums and media for those whose experience in peacework deserve the amplifications and textured ruminations of poetry. Though *Come Together: Imagine Peace* does not archive the contexts in which these poems came into being, or how they might continue to circulate—not just on email or in readings, but on walls and in streets—we invite poets to celebrate and record those deployments of language for peace. In *Behind the Lines: War Resistance Poetry on the American Homefront, since 1941,* I concluded with an exhortation for poets to continue to participate in this often-quixotic making and movement:

> In this making, in this composing, in this movement-building, we know that our actions will not necessarily lead to immediate change, and may never end war; yet, we ought to remember that when we resist war, we are participating in something that many people throughout history have struggled for, even given their lives for. Since war will not soon be sloughed off as a vestigial organ or an archaism, war resistance will survive and persist—even thrive—because poets continue to articulate, question, motivate and sustain it—in the symbolic action of their utterances and in the prose of their daily involvement making resistance. A visionary aspect of the peace movement, war resistance poems valorize the struggle inherent in resistance and argue against the mythologies of pro-war discourse so that, when the next wars come, people will resist the manufacture of public consent.... This is a fight worth writing for, and the lines made and broken are part of "millions of intricate moves," whose sentence might end with the word *peace.*

Epilogue

What strikes me now, with our nation still mired in two wars, is how much our own self-argument can come to silence us, and how we can become victims of our own narratives of despair. The poems of *Come Together: Imagine Peace* remind us that, though the work of peacemaking is never done, and though we face the most powerful forces in the world, we are not alone, and our voices bear the burden of the silenced throughout the globe. As Rebecca Solnit recently wrote:

> What does it mean to be radical, to tell radical stories in our time, to win the battle of the story? The North American tradition seems to focus its activity on the exposé, the telling of the grim underside of what we know: the food is poison, the system is corrupt, the leaders are lying, the war is failing. There is a place for this, but you cannot base a revolution on the bad things the status quo forgot to mention. You need to tell the stories they are not telling, to learn to see where they are blind, to look at how the great changes of the world come from the shadows and the margins, not center stage, to see where we're winning and that we can win something that matters, if not everything all the time.

The work of peacemaking, and the work of peace poetry, is at least in part to give voice to those small victories—where no blood was spilled, but lives were changed, justice was won, and peace was forged, achieved, or found. And words bring us there, to the brink of something new. Peace poetry is larger than a moral injunction against war; it is an articulation of the expanse, the horizon where we might come together. To adapt a line by the Sufi poet Rumi: *Beyond the realm of good and evil, there is a field.*

— Philip Metres (September 2008)

Some Precedents

"Some say a host of horsemen..."   **Sappho**

Some say a host of horsemen, some say warriors,
Some say a fleet of ships is the loveliest
Vision on this dark earth, but I say it's
The one you love most.

It's easy to make this clear—
Since Helen, who outshone
Everyone in beauty, abandoned
A good husband

And sailed for Troy
Without a thought
For her dear daughter, her parents
Led astray [   ]
[   ]
[   ] so quickly [   ]

It reminds me of Anaktoria—
I'd rather see her vivacious walk
And the flicker of light on her face
Than all the Lydian chariots and armies arrayed before us.

(Adapted by Philip Metres)

As I Ponder'd in Silence — Walt Whitman

As I ponder'd in silence,
Returning upon my poems, considering, lingering long,
A Phantom arose before me, with distrustful aspect,
Terrible in beauty, age, and power,
The genius of poets of old lands,
As to me directing like flame its eyes,
With finger pointing to many immortal songs,
And menacing voice, *What singest thou?* it said;
Know'st thou not, there is but one theme for ever-enduring bards?
And that is the theme of War, the fortune of battles,
The making of perfect soldiers?

Be it so, then I answer'd,
I too, haughty Shade, also sing war—and a longer and greater
        one than any,
Waged in my book with varying fortune—with flight, advance,
        and retreat—Victory deferr'd and wavering,
(Yet, methinks, certain, or as good as certain, at the last,)—The
        field the world;
For life and death—for the Body, and for the eternal Soul,
Lo! too am come, chanting the chant of battles,
I, above all, promote brave soldiers.

Poem #739 — Emily Dickinson

I many times thought Peace had come
When Peace was far away—
As Wrecked Men—deem they sight the Land—
At Centre of the Sea—

And struggle slacker—but to prove
As hopelessly as I—
How many the fictitious Shores—
Before the Harbor be—

Conscientious Objector   Edna St. Vincent Millay

I shall die, but that is all that I shall do for Death.
I hear him leading his horse out of the stall; I hear the clatter on
     the barn-floor.
He is in haste; he has business in Cuba, business in the Balkans,
     many calls to make this morning.
But I will not hold the bridle while he clinches the girth.
And he may mount by himself: I will not give him a leg up.

Though he flick my shoulders with his whip, I will not tell him
     which way the fox ran.
With his hoof on my breast, I will not tell him where the black
     boy hides in the swamp.
I shall die, but that is all that I shall do for Death; I am not on
     his pay-roll.

I will not tell him the whereabout of my friends nor of my
     enemies either.
Though he promise me much, I will not map him the route to
     any man's door.
Am I a spy in the land of the living, that I should deliver men to
     Death?
Brother, the password and the plans of our city are safe with me;
     never through me
Shall you be overcome.

Waiting for the Barbarians   C. P. Cavafy
translated by Edmund Keeley & Philip Sherrard

What are we waiting for, assembled in the forum?

     The barbarians are due here today.

Why isn't anything happening in the senate?
Why do the senators sit there without legislating?

     Because the barbarians are coming today.
     What laws can the senators make now?

Once the barbarians are here, they'll do the legislating.

Why did our emperor get up so early,
and why is he sitting at the city's main gate
on his throne, in state, wearing the crown?

   Because the barbarians are coming today
   and the emperor is waiting to receive their leader.

He has even prepared a scroll to give him,
replete with titles, with imposing names.
Why have our two consuls and praetors come out today
wearing their embroidered, their scarlet togas?
Why have they put on bracelets with so many amethysts,
and rings sparkling with magnificent emeralds?
Why are they carrying elegant canes
beautifully worked in silver and gold?

   Because the barbarians are coming today
   and things like that dazzle the barbarians.

Why don't our distinguished orators come forward as usual
to make their speeches, say what they have to say?

   Because the barbarians are coming today
   and they're bored by rhetoric and public speaking.

Why this sudden restlessness, this confusion?
(How serious people's faces have become.)
Why are the streets and squares emptying so rapidly,
everyone going home so lost in thought?

   Because night has fallen and the barbarians have not
come.
   And some who have just returned from the border say
   there are no barbarians any longer.

And now, what's going to happen to us without barbarians?
They were, those people, a kind of solution.

Creation   **Kenneth Patchen**

Wherever the dead are there they are and
Nothing more. But you and I can expect
To see angels in the meadowgrass that look
Like cows—
And wherever we are in paradise
          in furnished room without bath and
          six flights up
Is all God! We read
To one another, loving the sound of the s's
Slipping up on the f's and much is good
Enough to raise the hair on our heads, like
          Rilke and Owen.

Any person who loves another person,
Wherever in the world, is with us in this room—
          even though there are battlefields.

August 22, 1939   Kenneth Rexroth

*". . . when you want to distract your mother from the discouraging
soulness, I will tell you what I used to do. To take her for a long walk in
the quiet country, gathering wildflowers here and there, resting under
the shade of trees, between the harmony of the vivid stream and the
tranquillity of the mother-nature, and I am sure she will enjoy this very
much, as you surely will be happy for it. But remember always, Dante,
in the play of happiness, don't use all for yourself only, but down
yourself just one step, at your side and help the weak ones that cry for
help, help the prosecuted and the victim; because they are your friends;
they are the comrades that fight and fall as your father and Bartolo
fought and fell yesterday, for the conquest of the joy of freedom for all
and the poor workers. In this struggle of life you will find more love and
you will be loved."*

—Nicola Sacco to his son Dante, Aug. 18, 1927

Angst und Gestalt und Gebet —Rilke

What is it all for, this poetry,
This bundle of accomplishment
Put together with so much pain?
Twenty years at hard labor,
Lessons learned from Li Po and Dante,
Indian chants and gestalt psychology;
What words can it spell,
This alphabet of one sensibility?
The pure pattern of the stars in orderly progression,
The thin air of fourteen-thousand-foot summits,
Their Pisgah views into what secrets of the personality,
The fire of poppies in eroded fields,
The sleep of lynxes in the noonday forest,
The curious anastomosis of the webs of thought,
Life streaming ungovernably away,
And the deep hope of man.
The centuries have changed little in this art,
The subjects are still the same.
"For Christ's sake take off your clothes and get into bed,
We are not going to live forever."
"Petals fall from the rose,"
We fall from life,
Values fall from history like men from shellfire,
Only a minimum survives,

Only an unknown achievement.
They can put it all on the headstones,
In all the battlefields,
"Poor guy, he never knew what it was all about."
Spectacled men will come with shovels in a thousand years,
Give lectures in universities on cultural advances, cultural lags.
A little more garlic in the soup,
A half-hour more in bed in the morning,
Some of them got it, some of them didn't;
The things they dropped in their hurry
Are behind the glass cases of dusky museums.
This year we made four major ascents,
Camped for two weeks at timberline,
Watched Mars swim close to the earth,
Watched the black aurora of war
Spread over the sky of a decayed civilization.
These are the last terrible years of authority.
The disease has reached its crisis,
Ten thousand years of power,
The struggle of two laws,
The rule of iron and spilled blood,
The abiding solidarity of living blood and brain.
They are trapped, beleaguered, murderous,
If they line their cellars with cork
It is not to still the pistol shots,
It is to insulate the last words of the condemned.
"Liberty is the mother
Not the daughter of order."
"Not the government of men
But the administration of things."
"From each according to his ability,
Unto each according to his needs."
We could still hear them,
Cutting steps in the blue ice of hanging glaciers,
Teetering along shattered arêtes.
The cold and cruel apathy of mountains
Has been subdued with a few strands of rope
And some flimsy iceaxes,
There are only a few peaks left.
Twenty-five years have gone since my first sweetheart.
Back from the mountains there is a letter waiting for me.

"I read your poem in the *New Republic*.
Do you remember the undertaker's on the corner,
How we peeped in the basement window at a sheeted figure
And ran away screaming? Do you remember?
There is a filling station on the corner,
A parking lot where your house used to be,
Only ours and two other houses are left.
We stick it out in the noise and carbon monoxide."
It was a poem of homesickness and exile,
Twenty-five years wandering around
In a world of noise and poison.
She stuck it out, I never went back,
But there are domestic as well as imported
Explosions and poison gases.
Dante was homesick, the Chinese made an art of it,
So was Ovid and many others,
Pound and Eliot amongst them,
Kropotkin dying of hunger,
Berkman by his own hand,
Fanny Baron biting her executioners,
Mahkno in the odor of calumny,
Trotsky, too, I suppose, passionately, after his fashion.
Do you remember?
What is it all for, this poetry,
This bundle of accomplishment
Put together with so much pain?
Do you remember the corpse in the basement?
What are we doing at the turn of our years,
Writers and readers of the liberal weeklies?

The Conscientious Objector   Karl Shapiro

The gates clanged and they walked you into jail
More tense than felons but relieved to find
The hostile world shut out, the flags that dripped
From every mother's windowpane, obscene
The bloodlust sweating from the public heart,
The dog authority slavering at your throat.
A sense of quiet, of pulling down the blind
Possessed you. Punishment you felt was clean.

The decks, the catwalks, and the narrow light
Composed a ship. This was a mutinous crew
Troubling the captains for plain decencies,
A Mayflower brim with pilgrims headed out
To establish new theocracies to west,
A Noah's ark coasting the topmost seas
Ten miles above the sodomites and fish.
These inmates loved the only living doves.

Like all men hunted from the world you made
A good community, voyaging the storm
To no safe Plymouth or green Ararat;
Trouble or calm, the men with Bibles prayed,
The gaunt politicals construed our hate.
The opposite of all armies, you were best
Opposing uniformity and yourselves;
Prison and personality were your fate.

You suffered not so physically but knew
Maltreatment, hunger, ennui of the mind.
Well might the soldier kissing the hot beach
Erupting in his face damn all your kind.
Yet you who saved neither yourselves nor us
Are equally with those who shed the blood
The heroes of our cause. Your conscience is
What we come back to in the armistice.

Fall 1961   Robert Lowell

Back and forth, back and forth
goes the tock, tock, tock
of the orange, bland, ambassadorial
face of the moon
on the grandfather clock.

All autumn, the chafe and jar
of nuclear war;
we have talked our extinction to death.
I swim like a minnow
behind my studio window.

Our end drifts nearer,
the moon lifts,
radiant with terror.
The state
is a diver under a glass bell.

A father's no shield
for his child.
We are like a lot of wild
spiders crying together,
but without tears.

Nature holds up a mirror.
One swallow makes a summer.
It's easy to tick
off the minutes,
but the clock hands stick.

Back and forth!
Back and forth, back and forth—
my one point of rest
is the orange and black
oriole's swinging nest!

For No Clear Reason   Robert Creeley

I dreamt last night
the fright was over, that
the dust came, and then water,
and women and men, together
again, and all was quiet
in the dim moon's light.

A paean of such patience—
laughing, laughing at me,
and the days extend over
the earth's great cover,
grass, trees, and flower-
ing season, for no clear reason.

Poem   Muriel Rukeyser

I lived in the first century of world wars.
Most mornings I would be more or less insane.
The newspapers would arrive with their careless stories,
The news would pour out of various devices
Interrupted by attempts to sell products to the unseen.
I would call my friends on other devices;
They would be more or less mad for similar reasons.
Slowly I would get to pen and paper,
Make my poems for others unseen and unborn.
In the day I would be reminded of those men and women,
Brave, setting up signals across vast distances,
Considering a nameless way of living, of almost unimagined
        values.
As the lights darkened, as the lights of night brightened,
We would try to imagine them, try to find each other,
To construct peace, to make love, to reconcile
Waking with sleeping, ourselves with each other,
Ourselves with ourselves. We would try by any means
To reach the limits of ourselves, to reach beyond ourselves,
To let go the means, to wake.

I lived in the first century of these wars.

At the Un-National Monument Along the Canadian Border

William Stafford

This is the field where the battle did not happen,
where the unknown soldier did not die.
This is the field where grass joined hands,
where no monument stands,
and the only heroic thing is the sky.

Birds fly here without any sound,
unfolding their wings across the open.
No people killed—or were killed—on this ground
hallowed by neglect and an air so tame
that people celebrate it by forgetting its name.

Watching the Jet Planes Dive

William Stafford

We must go back and find a trail on the ground
back of the forest and mountain on the slow land;
we must begin to circle on the intricate sod.
By such wild beginnings without help we may find
the small trail on through the buffalo-bean vines.

We must go back with noses and the palms of our hands,
and climb over the map in far places, everywhere,
and lie down whenever there is doubt and sleep there.
If roads are unconnected we must make a path,
no matter how far it is, or how lowly we arrive.

We must find something forgotten by everyone alive,
and make some fabulous gesture when the sun goes down
as they do by custom in little Mexico towns
where they crawl for some ritual up a rocky steep.
The jet planes dive; we must travel on our knees.

Peace Walk   William Stafford

We wondered what our walk should mean,
taking that un-march quietly;
the sun stared at our signs—"Thou shalt not kill."

Men by a tavern said, "Those foreigners..."
to a woman with a fur, who turned away—
like an elevator going down, their look at us.

Along a curb, their signs lined across,
a picket line stopped and stared
the whole width of the street, at ours: "Unfair."

Above our heads the sound truck blared—
by the park, under the autumn trees—
it said that love could fill the atmosphere:

Occur, slow the other fallout, unseen,
on islands everywhere—fallout, falling
unheard. We held our poster up to shade our eyes.

At the end we just walked away;
no one was there to tell us where to leave the signs.

Making Peace   Denise Levertov

A voice from the dark called out,
"The poets must give us
imagination of peace, to oust the intense, familiar
imagination of disaster. Peace, not only
the absence of war."

But peace, like a poem,
is not there ahead of itself,
can't be imagined before it is made,
can't be known except
in the words of its making,

grammar of justice,
syntax of mutual aid.

A feeling towards it,
dimly sensing a rhythm, is all we have
until we begin to utter its metaphors,
learning them as we speak.

A line of peace might appear
if we restructured the sentence our lives are making,
revoked its reaffirmation of profit and power,
questioned our needs, allowed
long pauses. . . .

A cadence of peace might balance its weight
on that different fulcrum; peace, a presence,
an energy field more intense than war,
might pulse then,
stanza by stanza into the world,
each act of living
one of its words, each word
a vibration of light—facets
of the forming crystal.

The Altars in the Street   Denise Levertov

> *On June 17th, 1966, The New York Times reported that, as
> part of the Buddhist campaign of non-violent resistance,
> Viet-Namese children were building altars in the streets of
> Saigon and Hue, effectively jamming traffic.*

Children begin at green dawn nimbly to build
topheavy altars, overweighted with prayers,
thronged each instant more densely

with almost-visible ancestors.
Where tanks have cracked the roadway
the frail altars shake; here a boy

with red stumps for hands steadies a corner,
here one adjusts with his crutch the holy base.
The vast silence of Buddha overtakes

and overrules the oncoming roar
of tragic life that fills alleys and avenues;
it blocks the way of pedicabs, police, convoys.

The hale and maimed together
hurry to construct for the Buddha
a dwelling at each intersection. Each altar

made from whatever stones, sticks, dreams, are at hand,
is a facet of one altar; by noon
the whole city in all its corruption,

all its shed blood the monsoon cannot wash away,
has become a temple,
fragile, insolent, absolute.

From Wichita Vortex Sutra   **Allen Ginsberg**

I call all Powers of imagination
        to my side in this auto to make Prophecy,
                        all Lords
            of human kingdoms to come
Shambu Bharti Baba naked covered with ash
            Khaki Baba fat-bellied mad with the dogs
Dehorahava Baba who moans Oh how wounded, How wounded
        Sitaram Onkar Das Thakur who commands
                        give up your desire
Satyananda who raises two thumbs in tranquility
            Kali Pada Guha Roy whose yoga drops before the void
                Shivananda who touches the breast and says OM
Srimata Krishnaji of Brindaban who says take for your guru
            William Blake the invisible father of English visions
            Sri Ramakrishna master of ecstasy eyes
                half closed who only cries for his mother

Chaitanya arms upraised singing & dancing his own praise
    merciful Chango judging our bodies
        Durga-Ma covered with blood
            destroyer of battlefield illusions
        million-faced Tathagata gone past suffering
    Preserver Harekrishna returning in the age of pain
Sacred Heart my Christ acceptable
        Allah the Compassionate One
           Jahweh Righteous One
        all Knowledge-Princes of Earth-man, all
    ancient Seraphim of heavenly Desire, Devas, yogis
        & holymen I chant to—
        Come to my lone presence
            into this Vortex named Kansas,
I lift my voice aloud,
    make Mantra of American language now,
        I here declare the end of the War!
        Ancient days' Illusion!
    and pronounce words beginning my own millennium.
Let the States tremble,
    let the Nation weep,
        let Congress legislate its own delight
           let the President execute his own desire—
this Act done by my own voice,
        nameless Mystery—
published to my own senses,
        blissfully received by my own form
    approved with pleasure by my sensations
    manifestation of my very thought
    accomplished in my own imagination
        all realms within my consciousness fulfilled

A Litany for Survival   Audre Lorde

For those of us who live at the shoreline
standing upon the constant edges of decision
crucial and alone
for those of us who cannot indulge
the passing dreams of choice
who love in doorways coming and going

in the hours between dawns
looking inward and outward
at once before and after
seeking a now that can breed
futures
like bread in our children's mouths
so their dreams will not reflect
the death of ours:

For those of us
who were imprinted with fear
like a faint line in the center of our foreheads
learning to be afraid with our mother's milk
for by this weapon
this illusion of some safety to be found
the heavy-footed hoped to silence us
For all of us
this instant and this triumph
We were never meant to survive.

And when the sun rises we are afraid
it might not remain
when the sun sets we are afraid
it might not rise in the morning
when our stomachs are full we are afraid
of indigestion
when our stomachs are empty we are afraid
we may never eat again
when we are loved we are afraid
love will vanish
when we are alone we are afraid
love will never return
and when we speak we are afraid
our words will not be heard
nor welcomed
but when we are silent
we are still afraid

So it is better to speak
remembering
we were never meant to survive

The Bombing of Baghdad   June Jordan

I

began and did not terminate for 42 days
and 42 nights relentless minute after minute
more than 110,000 times
we bombed Iraq we bombed Baghdad
we bombed Basra/we bombed military
installations we bombed the National Museum
we bombed schools we bombed air raid
shelters we bombed water we bombed
electricity we bombed hospitals we
bombed streets we bombed highways
we bombed everything that moved/we
bombed everything that did not move we
bombed Baghdad
a city of 5.5 million human beings
we bombed radio towers we bombed
telephone poles we bombed mosques
we bombed runways we bombed tanks
we bombed trucks we bombed cars we bombed bridges
we bombed the darkness we bombed
the sunlight we bombed them and we
bombed them and we cluster bombed the citizens
of Iraq and we sulfur bombed the citizens of Iraq
and we napalm bombed the citizens of Iraq and we
complemented these bombings/these "sorties" with
Tomahawk cruise missiles which we shot
repeatedly by the thousands upon thousands
into Iraq
(you understand an Iraqi Scud missile
is *quote* militarily insignificant *unquote* and we
do not mess around with insignificant)
so we used cruise missiles repeatedly
we fired them into Iraq
And I am not pleased
I am not very pleased
None of this fits into my notion of "things going very
well"

II

The bombing of Baghdad
did not obliterate the distance or the time
between my body and the breath
of my beloved

III

This was Custer's Next-To-Last Stand
I hear Crazy Horse singing as he dies
I dedicate myself to learn that song
I hear that music in the moaning of the Arab world

IV

Custer got accustomed to just doing his job
Pushing westward into glory
Making promises
Searching for the savages/their fragile
Temporary settlements
For raising children/dancing down the rain/and praying
For the mercy of a heard of buffalo
Custer/he pursued these savages
He attacked at dawn
He murdered the men/murdered the boys
He captured the women and converted
them (I'm sure)
to his religion
Oh, how gently did he bid his darling fiancée
farewell!
How sweet the gaze her eyes bestowed upon her warrior!
Loaded with guns and gunpowder he embraced
the guts and gore of manifest white destiny
He pushed westward
to annihilate the savages
("Attack at dawn!")
and seize their territories
        seize their women
        seize their natural wealth

V

And I am cheering for the arrows
and the braves

VI

And all who believed some must die
they were already dead
And all who believe only they possess
human being and therefore human rights
they no longer stood among the possibly humane
And all who believed that retaliation/revenge/defense
derive from God-given prerogatives of white men
And all who believed that waging war is anything
        beside terrorist activity in the first
        place and in the last
And all who believed that F-15's/F-16's/"Apache"
        helicopters/
B-52 bombers/smart bombs/dumb bombs/napalm/artillery/
battleships/nuclear warheads amount to anything other
than terrorist tools of a terrorist undertaking
And all who believed that holocaust means something
        that happens only to white people
And all who believed that Desert Storm
        signified anything besides the delivery of an American
        holocaust against the peoples of the Middle East
All who believed these things
they were already dead
They no longer stood among the possibly humane

And this is for Crazy Horse singing as he dies
because I live inside his grave
And this is for the victims of the bombing of Baghdad
because the enemy traveled from my house
                to blast your homeland
                into pieces of children
                into pieces of sand

And in the aftermath of carnage
perpetrated in my name

how should I dare to offer you my hand
how shall I negotiate the implications
            of my shame?

My heart cannot confront
this death without relief
My soul will not control
this leaking of my grief

And this is for Crazy Horse singing as he dies
And here is my song of the living
who must sing against the dying
sing to join the living
with the dead

Wildpeace   Yehuda Amichai

Not the peace of a cease-fire
not even the vision of the wolf and the lamb,
but rather
as in the heart when the excitement is over
and you can talk only about a great weariness.
I know that I know how to kill,
that makes me an adult.
And my son plays with a toy gun that knows
how to open and close its eyes and say Mama.
A peace
without the big noise of beating swords into ploughshares,
without words, without
the thud of the heavy rubber stamp: let it be
light, floating, like lazy white foam.
A little rest for the wounds—
who speaks of healing?
(And the howl of the orphans is passed from one generation
to the next, as in a relay race:
the baton never falls.)

Let it come
like wildflowers,
suddenly, because the field
must have it: wildpeace.

From "State of Siege"   **Mahmoud Darwish**

Salaam upon whoever splits with me the attention to
light's ecstasy, the butterfly light, in
this tunnel's night!

        *

Salaam upon whoever shares with me my glass
in the density of a night that overflows two seats:
salaam upon my ghost!

        *

Salaam is what a traveler says to himself
to another traveler on the other side . . .

Salaam is the doves of two strangers sharing their last
cooing, on the edge of the chasm

        *

Salaam is two enemies longing, each separately,
to yawn on boredom's sidewalk

Salaam is two lovers moaning to bathe
in moonlight

        *

Salaam is the apology of the mighty to the one
with weaker weapons and stronger range

Salaam is the sword breaking in front of natural
beauty, where dew smelts the iron

        *

Salaam is a friendly day, pleasant, light-
footed, enemy of no one

Salaam is a train that unites all its passengers
who are coming from or going to a picnic in eternity's suburbs

*

Salaam is the public confession of truth:
What have you done with the murdered's ghost?

Salaam is the turning toward an errand in the garden:
What will we plant in a little while?

*

Salaam is the caution against a fox's attractive
eyes that lure the instinct of a frightened woman

Salaam is the ah strutting the crescendo
of a muwashah, in the heart of a bleeding guitar

*

Salaam is the lament of a young man whose heart a woman's
    beauty
mark pierced, not a bullet or a bomb

Salaam is the singing of life here, in life,
on the string of an ear of wheat

The Story So Far:

Poems of Witness & Elegy

The Story So Far

Shara McCallum

To choose a son for sacrifice
the war continues:

after four thousand years
Isaac and Ishmael still clamouring for God's ear.

In the light of day's end, in a warehouse in Rwanda,
a Hutu foreman hovers over one of his workers,

a pregnant Tutsi woman. This ordinary man
with a wife, children of his own,

will disembowel her. Not a stranger
but this woman he knows. To *learn*—

as later, in his defense, he will confess—
what the inside of a Tutsi woman is like.

On the radio, a young woman recounts her tale
of the Cambodian killing fields:

rice paddies, thatched hut where she plays,
men coming for her father first,

her mother orphaning her so she might survive.
This child eating crickets and coal to stay alive.

Butterflies by the hundreds alight on her face,
cover each inch of skin, their furred wings

opening and closing
against her eyelids, lips, and cheeks.

Told in any language—the parables of suffering,
the fractured syllables of loss,

the space in the back of a throat
still longing to sound the names of God.

Requiem for the Buddhas of Bamiyan   Karen Kovacik

> If we gain something, it was there from the beginning.
> If we lose something, it is hidden nearby.
>   —Ryokan

Between the empire of China
    and the empire of Rome,
in an oasis along the Silk Road,

you heard pomegranates change hands
    in Latin and Farsi and Greek.
Chinese generals, Persian merchants,

inventors of gunpowder and algebra,
    fanciers of rhubarb and bronze:
all conducted their commerce

in your shadow: you
    who saw monasteries cut from mountains,
you who were sculpted out of sandstone,

who listened to the whispers of Christians;
    who welcomed Muslims and Manicheans,
disciples of Nestor and Zoroaster.

Leopards and lions rolled past you
    in their cages, actors
mimicked peacocks and parrots, travelers

who'd thirsted through the Taklamakan Desert
    gave thanks to plural gods.
You who survived Genghis Khan's cannon,

who saw the British retreat, then Soviets and Americans,
    you whom the Taliban ringed
with burning tires, blackening your face,

you with dynamite in your groin, you witness
    to starving farmers, to secret schools for girls:
for fourteen centuries you stood fast

still as Siddhartha
     on the night of his enlightenment,
as much a part of this valley as the wind.

Who will know you now by your absence,
     remembering your before?
When the night comes, who will know you?

When the ash falls, who will know you?
     After earthquakes and eclipses,
wherever there is fire,

how to feel you filling us and leaving us,
     abiding in the grottoes
of our breath?

The End and the Beginning

Wislawa Szymborska
Trans. Joanna Trzeciak

After every war
someone has to clean up.
Things won't
straighten themselves up, after all.

Someone has to push the rubble
to the side of the road,
so the corpse-filled wagons
can pass.

Someone has to get mired
in scum and ashes,
sofa springs,
splintered glass,
and bloody rags.

Someone must drag in a girder
to prop up a wall,
Someone must glaze a window,
rehang a door.

Photogenic it's not,
and takes years.
All the cameras have left
for another war.

We'll need bridges back
and new railway stations.
Sleeves will go ragged
from rolling them up.

Someone, broom in hand,
still recalls how it was.
Someone else listens
and nods with unsevered head.
But already there are those nearby
starting to mill about
who will find it dull.

From out of the bushes
sometimes someone still unearths
rusted-out arguments
and carries them to the garbage pile.

Those who knew
what was going on here
must make way to
those who know little.
And less than little.
And finally as little as nothing.

In the grass which has overgrown
causes and effects,
someone must be stretched out
blade of grass in his mouth
gazing at the clouds.

At the Museum of Archaeology   Jon Volkmer

Yahweh is a god of the hills, but he is not,
the Arameans say, a god of the valleys.
This much is quoted from 1 Kings

on the museum wall, but not
the verses that follow, where
one hundred thousand are smitten

for holding this opinion. Of those
who flee, twenty-seven thousand perish
beneath the walls of Aphek. Among

the dead, we may guess: El, the creator,
his consort Athirat, the storm god
Ba'al, his huntress sister Anat.

So many soldiers and dieties dead—
even the lexicon was laid waste.
Me with my fancy degrees, and I never knew,

never had a clue, there was a word
for worshipping one god while
respecting the realms of others.

Iron trinkets, sand figurines,
a glass case in an empty room:
the usual leavings of monolatry.

Willows   Maj Ragain

Blessed are Those Who Mourn
—Norman O. Brown

It was the mid nineteen forties.
The war was on the other side
of the ocean. I was five years old.
No school yet, couldn't read or write.
My grandparents' farm was my home that summer.
I wandered the fencerows,
the boundaries at the wood's edge.
Even then the puzzle was forming:
why everyone I knew was hiding
something, coloring in the empty spaces
the way I did with my crayons.
I had not yet felt the weight
of the world's heart,
but I could hear
its drum beat in my chest.

One summer noon, my grandma Blanche
packed a picnic basket. We found shade
beneath the willows along the branch
meandering through the pasture.
I played in the green tresses hanging
into the ankle deep water sparkling its way
over sand and pebbles. The half dozen willows
leaned against one another, whispering in the heat,
old women still green from their tears.
Grandma called them *weeping willows*.
I heard her say *weeping widows*.
No, she smiled, *It's willows*.

Now, after all these years, count sixty,
I am certain it is *weeping widows*.

(March 9, 2008)

Bones of a Crow   Jack McGuane

Home from the Navy after the war,
out in the woods one day I shot a crow.
He fell straight down
a shapeless heap of blood,
beak, black feathers,
one baleful eye.

In that unexpected instant
another predator died too.
I wished I could take back
the 00 buckshot
that tore him apart.
I couldn't bring myself
to touch his body.

As I float down now
into the old neighborhood
fifty years later,
I notice at first that I've outlived
three sugar maples my father planted
the year I was born.

Someone vinyl-sided our house.
My parents saved for years
to afford asbestos shingles
from Johns Manville,
the latest thing in 1937.
We were the second house
to have them I remember.

A new subdivision crowds out
the sassafras and wild huckleberry
in those woods across the road.
Down by the railroad trestle,
a huge concrete pipe lies
where we used to skinny-dip
in Doxey's Brook.

Four blocks up DuBois Ave.

a Seven-Eleven
displaces Warnken's Grocery,
where I landed my first job at fourteen
delivering phoned-in orders.
I saved tips for two years
to buy that shotgun.
After the crow died
I would have given back the gun
if he could still be alive.

But, the neighborhood moved on
and so did I, eventually,
and the bones of the crow
are buried now
under one of the new houses.

Still—I sometimes wonder—
lying out there in the woods like that
how long does it take for time
and seasons and the patient rain
to carry off a tortured memory

E Mail Message   Lyn Lifshin

"I love the idea of you
putting quilts on your
plants, a yard of quilts
like a front-yard bed
and you tucking in your
plants for naps." The
just turned earth, your
just turned earth. You
won't need a quilt,
you never like any-
thing too near the foot
that was mangled. The
other, buried in Nam.
I tucked the basil in,
covered cilantro and

chives, the wind a
lullaby getting some-
thing ready for sleep or
dying, really the same
holding and wrapping
as the dark grows

True Peace   Sam Hamill

Half broken on that smoky night,
hunched over sake in a serviceman's dive
somewhere in Naha, Okinawa,
nearly fifty years ago,

I read of the Saigon Buddhist monks
who stopped the traffic on a downtown thoroughfare
so their master, Thich Quang Dúc, could take up
the lotus posture in the middle of the street.
And they baptized him there with gas
and kerosene, and he struck a match
and burst into flame.

That was June, nineteen-sixty-three,
and I was twenty, a U.S. Marine.

The master did not move, did not squirm,
he did not scream
in pain as his body was consumed.

Neither child nor yet a man,
I wondered to my Okinawan friend,
what can it possibly mean
to make such a sacrifice, to give one's life
with such horror, but with dignity and conviction.
How can any man endure such pain
and never cry and never blink.

And my friend said simply, "Thich Quang Dúc
had achieved true peace."

And I knew that night true peace
for me would never come.
Not for me, Nirvana. This suffering world
is mine, mine to suffer in its grief.

Half a century later, I think
of Bô Tát Thich Quang Dúc,
revered as a bodhisattva now—his lifetime
building temples, teaching peace,
and of his death and the statement that it made.

Like Shelley's, his heart refused to burn,
even when they burned his ashes once again
in the crematorium—his generous heart
turned magically to stone.

What is true peace, I cannot know.
A hundred wars have come and gone
as I've grown old. I bear their burdens in my bones.
Mine's the heart that burns
today, mine the thirst, the hunger in the soul.

Old master, old teacher,
what is it that I've learned?

Why I Wrote Out by Hand Ronald Johnson's *The Book of the Green Man* On An Autumn Evening in 1970

Jeanne Shannon

September. The equinox, dark coming early
and a bronze rain falling.

> *of the seasons,*
> *seamless,*
> *a garland*

> *Solstice*
> *to equinox—days,*

> *come full circle*

I am at work, though it is evening. I am
typing a briefing for the Air Force.
Tomorrow the Colonel will take these
words to Washington and offer them to
Congress.

> Carefully
> the Colonel
> writes downs his litanies:

> > the B-1 bomber,
> > first strike,
> > survivability

> as if they were
> prayers to the gods of war.

> While he composes another page
> I wait
> and copy Johnson's litanies
> to other gods

> his songs of vegetable gold,
> of white light

opening like flowers—
dog-violet, asphodel & celandine

a Celtic goddess clad in broom and oak-
flowers,
and the Green Man of Wales
at whose command birds sang

*

Because it is September,
because a bronze rain falls
upon the dark geometries
of houses

Because the talk around me is of bombs
and war

Because I want to *break out like fire and
wax greene*

Because I want
white nights
when darkness gets up and walks

Because I want
moon-glade and phosphorescence,
and all things *rich and glittering and
strange*

Because I want to think of rook and
worm
only one cycle out of many
and bee
its dust & honies

of *dazzle* written in the poplar leaves

Because I want
to walk in gardens
gone into earth these hundred years
Because I want

to tell the Colonel
of foliage planted in our veins

to say to him
                we stand in our rayed form

Because I want
to bring the poem into my body

to sing, note against note
its difficult
and radiant harmonies

       [All words in italics are quotations from *The Book
       of the Green Man*, © 1967 by Ronald Johnson.

Because One Is Always Forgotten   Carolyn Forché

*In Memoriam, José Rudolfo Viera
1939-1981, El Salvador*

When Viera was buried we knew it had come to an end,
his coffin rocking into the ground like a boat or a cradle;

I could take my heart, he said, and give it to a peasant
and he would cut it up and give it back:

you can't eat heart in those four dark
chambers where a man can be kept years.

A boy soldier in the bone-hot sun works his knife
to peel the face from a dead man

and hang it from the branch of a tree
flowering with such faces.

The heart is the toughest part of the body.
Tenderness is in the hands.

Bosnian Love Poem   John Bradley

In Memory of Bosko Brckic and Admira Ismic

He was a Serb, she a Muslim.
A Muslim and Serb in love

in the city of Sarajevo.
That's all we need to know.

The Serbs say the Muslims killed them.
The Muslims say the Serbs killed them.

Both sides had agreed to let Bosko and Admira pass
on Wednesday, at 4 pm. On Wednesday, at 4 pm.,

they died, on the Vrbana Bridge.
In the zone not Muslim nor Serb.

Shot at the same time, Bosko
died first, then Admira, holding him.

For six days, no one came near.
For six days, everyone watched.

Bosko, face down. Admira, left
arm across Bosko's back.

He, a Serb, she, a Muslim, embracing.
Everything we need to know.

Intelligent War Machine   David Sklar & Geoffrey A. Landis

And if I could, would I choose not to strike
This sleeping target, unaware?
Or must it always be my role to fight?
My program is to know, my flaw to care.

Ghazal: The Footbridge Over the Somes   Steve Wilson

Autumn arrives, with night perching on my open window.
I watch workers shuffle home, a foreigner at an open window.

When winter retreats, the melting ice reflects like glass—
I wander out. A women's robe hangs at a half-open window.

The river, alive beneath the bridge, swims over rocks, bottles,
an empty barrel. What words you whispered at your open
        window.

Years ago, armies took these streets. "Which side were you on?"
I ask Ferenc, my old neighbor. His face is an open window.

Beside one bank or the other, children play in the alleyways.
I'm alone, waving to ghosts through this open window.

—Cluj, Romania

911   Michael Salinger

hate is extremely flammable
its vapors may cause flash fire
hate is harmful if inhaled
keep hate away from heat, sparks and flame
do not breathe the vapors of hate
wash thoroughly after using hate
if you accidentally swallow hate
get medical attention

prejudice is an eye and skin irritant
its vapors too are harmful
do not get prejudice in eyes
or on clothing
prejudice is not recommended for use
by persons with heart conditions
if prejudice is swallowed, induce vomiting
if prejudice comes in contact with skin,

remove clothing and wash skin
if breathing is affected, get fresh air immediately

violence is harmful if absorbed through the skin
keep violence out of the reach of children
do not remain in enclosed areas
where violence is present
remove pets and birds from the vicinity of violence
cover aquariums to protect from violence
drift and run off from sites of violence
may be hazardous
this product is highly toxic
exposure to violence may cause
injury or death.

On A Sign Announcing: Joseph Ross
Expanding Arlington National Cemetery

The sign stands innocent as a smile.
Held aloft on two legs,
it is satisfied and confident,
announcing "Your tax dollars at work."
Expansion is progress. Growth is good.

It is clean and straight, this sign.
It is clear.
Placed by a competent caretaker—
no lean, no tilt, no doubt.
Its letters stare out at us,
no flourish, no curls,
efficient, laces tight.

Most signs in this cemetery
are solemn carvings in stone
or fatherly warnings against irreverence.
But this one brags,
like much of America: bigger is better.
In the past, this cemetery has expanded
with no publicity.

No need to remind the grieving
that even graveyards need to grow.

And this cemetery does grow
in bursts of gunfire.
Here, the green hills do not roll like waves,
they rattle as if covered by a blanket
woven from bones,
unfurled flat above this pregnant earth,
covering a cold it can never warm.

I walk through this place
where names and dates stare
from every direction:

old wars, new wars, wars to end all wars,
conventional wars, all manner of wars,
a war that took my neighbor,
a war that did not take my father.

I realize that I must step carefully here,
from road to grass,
I walk in this meadow where water is red
and I am brought back to other lawns—

I remember afternoons playing army,
running through front yards, hiding in my own,
rolling on grass that smelled like August,
crouching behind trees whose leaves
I had earlier raked.
In those days, when you were shot
you got to lie on your back
and watch the sunlight strain
through a heaven of green leaves,
then, after counting to twenty,
you could jump up and play again, of course.

But today, I stand still,
surrounded by a silent, gawking crowd.
They stare up from beneath
their white stones,

their teeth bared and straight,
their smiles long since gone.
I wonder what they think
of this sign of the times,
whose black and white letters
tell us, in a language we know too well,
that progress is tallied in tears.

History   Eric Pankey

A hundred flint arrowheads, chipped, rain-washed, scat-
        tered through a meadow of ragweed and clover,
The flesh they ripped, the rib nicked, the shields of horse-
        hide torn, all lost to the elements;
An ice-pierced daybreak through a mica screen and the first
        lute arrives in China from Persia;

The uses of ambergris are perfected; the lamb's blood dries
        above the doorway; a glacier calves an iceberg;
From the rock where a father offered up his son as sacrifice,
        the Prophet ascends into paradise;
The summer you step on a rusted nail, the willows green
        and bend to the river; the river floods;

Before nightfall, a body is bargained for, secreted away in a
        borrowed grave fashioned from a cave;
Again, walls and towers topple. And no language but grief
        is left in common. And grief is no language at all.
There is no history, only fits and starts, laughter at the
        table, lovers asleep, slaughter, the forgetfulness.

And yet for three nights straight, nothing but starlight—
        Byzantine, quicksilver, an emanation of a past—
And tonight you have renamed the constellations after
        the mudras: *The Gesture Beyond Mercy,*
The Gesture for Warding Off Evil, The Gesture of Fearlessness,
        The Gift-Bestowing Gesture of Compassion.

Call and Answer

Poems of Exhortation & Action

Call and Answer · Robert Bly

Tell me why it is we don't lift our voices these days
And cry over what is happening. Have you noticed
The plans are made for Iraq and the ice cap is melting?

I say to myself: "Go on, cry. What's the sense
Of being an adult and having no voice? Cry out!
See who will answer! This is Call and Answer!"

We will have to call especially loud to reach
Our angels, who are hard of hearing; they are hiding
In the jugs of silence filled during our wars.

Have we agreed to so many wars that we can't
Escape from silence? If we don't lift our voices, we allow
Others (who are ourselves) to rob the house.

How come we've listened to the great criers—Neruda,
Akhmatova, Thoreau, Frederick Douglass—and now
We're silent as sparrows in the little bushes?

Some masters say our life lasts only seven days.
Where are we in the week? Is it Thursday yet?
Hurry, cry now! Soon Sunday night will come.

[August 2002]

From "An Atlas of the Difficult World" · Adrienne Rich

XI

One night in Monterey Bay the death-freeze of the century:
a precise, detached caliper-grip holds the stats and the quarter-
          moon
in arrest: the hardiest plants crouch shrunken, a "killing frost"
on bougainvillea, Pride of Madeira, roseate black-purple
          succulents bowed
juices sucked awry in one orgy of freezing
slumping on their stems like old faces evicted from cheap hotels
—into the streets of the universe, now!

Earthquake and drought followed by freezing followed by war.
Flags are blossoming now where little else is blossoming
and I am bent on fathoming what it means to love my country.
The history of this earth and the bones within it?
Soils and cities, promises made and mocked, plowed contours
        of shame and of hope?
Loyalties, symbols, murmurs extinguished and echoing?
Grids of states stretching westward, underground waters?
Minerals, traces, rumors I am made from, morsel, miniscule
        fibre, one woman
like and unlike so many, fooled as to her destiny, the scope of
        her task?
One citizen like and unlike so many, touched and untouched
        in passing
—each of us now a driven grain, a nucleus, a city in crisis
some busy constructing enclosures, bunkers, to escape the
        common fate
some trying to revive dead statues to lead us, breathing their
        breath against marble lips
some who try to teach the moment, some who preach the moment
some who aggrandize, some who diminish themselves in the
        face of half-grasped events
—power and powerlessness run amuck, a tape reeling backward
        in jeering, screeching syllables—
some for whom war is new, others for whom it merely continues
        the old paroxysms of time
some marching for peace who for twenty years did not march
        for justice
some for whom peace is a white man's word and a white man's
        privilege
some who have learned to handle and contemplate the shapes
        of powerlessness and power
as the nurse learns hip and thigh and weight of the body he has
        to lift and sponge, day upon day
as she blows with her every skill on the spirit's embers still
        burning by their own laws in the bed of death.
A patriot is not a weapon. A patriot is one who wrestles for
        the soul of her country
as she wrestles for her own being, for the soul of his country

(gazing through the great circle at Window Rock into the sheen
    of the Viet Nam Wall)
as he wrestles for his own being. A patriot is a citizen trying to
    wake
from the burnt-out dream of innocence, the nightmare
of the white general and the Black general posed in their
    camouflage,
to remember her true country, remember his suffering land:
    remember
that blessing and cursing are born as twins and separated at
    birth and meet again in mourning
that the internal emigrant is the most homesick of all women
    and of all men
that every flag that flies today is a cry of pain.
    Where are we moored?
    What are the bindings?
    What behooves us?

(The Truth)   **William Heyen**

Across Brockport Village, a blight of orange & yellow ribbons
meant to remember our half-million participants
in "Operation Desert Storm," those who put their lives on line
to protect our country, as our president says.
Darkening ribbons encircle trees, telephone poles,
mailboxes, porch rails—so I was understandably half bored
& half nuts with war & ugliness, so climbed to my roof
& tied a large black configuration of bow & ribbons
to my aerial. Up there, I saw how it divides the winter sky
with its alphabet of one emotional letter, a vowel....

At first, no one noticed, but then a car turned around.
Later, a police cruiser slowed down, & then another.
A reporter stopped for that infamous photo that appeared in *Time*
& the first of a hundred interviews I respectfully declined,
& neighbors gathered. My phone kept ringing off the wall,
people yelling "bastard," & "traitor," & "get it the hell down,
or else."... Eventually, my best friend came to my door
& asked me why. I explained, "I can't explain." Others followed,

& insisted. "No comment," I said. "I don't want trouble,"
I said. "Read Hawthorne's 'The Minister's Black Veil.'"

I still like the way the black bow & ribbons flutter,
stark but suggestive of comic dark, serious, direct,
my own American allegiance & patriotic light.
Parson Hooper had his reasons, & half understood them,
but when he slept or spoke, his breath trembled the veil,
& even holy scripture seemed filtered by the terrible
transformation of black crepe into symbol. In the end,
not even his creator could commend the visionary parson
who espied the truth that separates & condemns.
Above my village, this beauty of black bow & ribbons.

Populist Manifesto No. 1   Lawrence Ferlinghetti

Poets, come out of your closets,
Open your windows, open your doors,
You have been holed-up too long
in your closed worlds.
Come down, come down
from your Russian Hills and Telegraph Hills,
your Beacon Hills and your Chapel Hills,
your Mount Analogues and Montparnasses,
down from your foothills and mountains,
out of your teepees and domes.
The trees are still falling
and we'll to the woods no more.
No time now for sitting in them
As man burns down his own house
to roast his pig
No more chanting Hare Krishna
while Rome burns.
San Francisco's burning,
Mayakovsky's Moscow's burning
the fossil-fuels of life.
Night & the Horse approaches
eating light, heat & power,
and the clouds have trousers.

No time now for the artist to hide
above, beyond, behind the scenes,
indifferent, paring his fingernails,
refining himself out of existence.
No time now for our little literary games,
no time now for our paranoias & hypochondrias,
no time now for fear & loathing,
time now only for light & love.
We have seen the best minds of our generation
destroyed by boredom at poetry readings.
Poetry isn't a secret society,
It isn't a temple either.
Secret words & chants won't do any longer.
The hour of oming is over,
the time of keening come,
a time for keening & rejoicing
over the coming end
of industrial civilization
which is bad for earth & Man.
Time now to face outward
in the full lotus position
with eyes wide open,
Time now to open your mouths
with a new open speech,
time now to communicate with all sentient beings,
All you 'Poets of the Cities'
hung in museums including myself,
All you poet's poets writing poetry
about poetry,
All you poetry workshop poets
in the boondock heart of America,
All you housebroken Ezra Pounds,
All you far-out freaked-out cut-up poets,
All you pre-stressed Concrete poets,
All you cunnilingual poets,
All you pay-toilet poets groaning with graffiti,
All you A-train swingers who never swing on birches,
All you masters of the sawmill haiku in the Siberias of America,
All you eyeless unrealists,
All you self-occulting supersurrealists,
All you bedroom visionaries and closet agitpropagators,

All you Groucho Marxist poets
and leisure-class Comrades
who lie around all day and talk about the workingclass
proletariat,
All you Catholic anarchists of poetry,
All you Black Mountaineers of poetry,
All you Boston Brahims and Bolinas bucolics,
All you den mothers of poetry,
All you zen brothers of poetry,
All you suicide lovers of poetry,
All you hairy professors of poesie,
All you poetry reviewers
drinking the blood of the poet,
All you Poetry Police—
Where are Whitman's wild children,
where the great voices speaking out
with a sense of sweetness and sublimity,
where the great new vision,
the great world-view,
the high prophetic song
of the immense earth
and all that sings in it
And our relations to it
Poets, descend
to the street of the world once more
And open your minds & eyes
with the old visual delight,
Clear your throat and speak up,
Poetry is dead, long live poetry
with terrible eyes and buffalo strength.
Don't wait for the Revolution
or it'll happen without you,
Stop mumbling and speak out
with a new wide-open poetry
with a new commonsensual 'public surface'
with other subjective levels
or other subversive levels,
a tuning fork in the inner ear
to strike below the surface.
Of your own sweet Self still sing
yet utter 'the word en-masse'

Poetry the common carrier
for the transportation of the public
to higher places
than other wheels can carry it.
Poetry still falls from the skies
into our streets still open.
They haven't put up the barricades, yet,
the streets still alive with faces,
lovely men & women still walking there,
still lovely creatures everywhere,
in the eyes of all the secret of all
still buried there,
Whitman's wild children still sleeping there,
Awake and walk in the open air.

Federal Building   Angele Ellis

I enter through security as taxpayer,
the needle's eye of citizenship. Bag on the table,
keys in a plastic container that could hold mail
or explosives. The only way in and out.
I remember with strained nostalgia
the protests of the eighties—
South Africa, Nicaragua, El Salvador,
the sit-ins at congressional offices,
the time we rode up and down the elevators
with our leaflets until the guards nabbed us
and threw us out. And that last time,
the sit-in during Desert Storm,
suspended between freedom and arrest,
swimming in ether like exotic fish
while our friends pressed against the aquarium glass
with hopeful signs
as if we could change history, levitate the building
like Abbie Hoffman tried with the Pentagon.
Now we are lucky to stand unmolested
on the public sidewalk,
the thin edge of the wedge of democracy.

For the Fifty   **Philip Metres**
(Who Made PEACE With Their Bodies)

In the green beginning,
    in the morning mist,
        they emerge from their chrysalis

of clothes: peel off purses & cells,
    slacks & Gap sweats, turtle-
        necks & tanks, Tommy's & Salvation

Army, platforms & clogs,
    abandoning bras and lingerie, labels
        & names, courtesies & shames,

the emperor's rhetoric of defense,
    laying it down, their child-
        stretched or still-taut flesh

giddy in sudden proximity,
    onto the cold earth: bodies fetal or supine,
        as if come-hithering

or dead, wriggle on the grass to form
    the shape of a word yet to come, almost
        embarrassing to name: a word

thicker, heavier than the rolled rags
    of their bodies seen from a cockpit:
        they touch to make

the word they want to become:
    it's difficult to get the news
        from our bodies, yet people die each day

for lack of what is found there:
    here: the fifty hold, & still
        to become a testament, a will,

embody something outside
    themselves & themselves: the body,
      the dreaming disarmed body.

Stupid Meditation on Peace   Robert Pinsky

    "He does not come to coo."
      —Gerard Manley Hopkins

Insomniac monkey-mind ponders the Dove,
Symbol not only of Peace but sexual
Love, the couple nestled and brooding.

After coupling, the human animal needs
The woman safe for nine months and more.
But the man after his turbulent minute or two

Is expendable. Usefully rash, reckless
For defense, in his void of redundancy
Willing to death and destruction.

Monkey-mind envies the male Dove
Who equally with the female secretes
Pigeon milk for the young from his throat.

For peace, send all human males between
Fourteen and twenty-five to school
On the Moon, or better yet Mars.

But women too are capable of Unpeace,
Yes, and we older men too, venom-throats.
Here's a great comic who says on our journey

We choose one of two tributaries: the River
Of Peace, or the River of Productivity.
The current of Art he says runs not between

Banks with birdsong in the fragrant shadows—
No, an artist must follow the stinks and rapids
Of the branch that drives the millstones and dynamos.

Is peace merely a vacuum, the negative
Of creation, or the absence of war?
The teaching says Peace is a positive energy.

Still something in me resists that sweet milk,
My mind resembles my restless, inferior cousin
Who fires his shit in handfuls from his cage.

The God of the Weather-Beaten Face   Martín Espada

for Camilo Mejía, conscientious objector

The gods gathered:
the crusader god took off his helmet,
the desert warrior god stood his shield in the corner,
the sword-maker god sat between them sharpening blades,
the bombardier god spread his maps on the table,
the god who collects infidel heads traded trophies
with the god who collects heathen scalps,
the god of gold opened his handkerchief
for the god of oil to wipe his dripping chin,
the god who punishes sin with boils scratched his boils
and called the meeting to order.

And the gods said: *War.*

Sergeant Mejía heard the prisoner moan under the hood
as the guards shoved him into a steel closet, then pounded
with a sledgehammer on the door until the moaning stopped;
heard machine-gun fire slicing heads from necks
with a roar that would be the envy of swords;
heard a soldier sobbing in the toilet for the headless boy
who would open his eyes every time the soldier closed his own.

Sometimes a song drifts up
through the moaning and sledgehammers,
machine guns and sobbing.
Sometimes a voice floats above pandemonium

the way a seagull floats over burning ships.
Sergeant Mejía heard his father's song,
the peasant mass of Nicaragua:
Vos sos el Dios de los pobres,
el Dios humano y sencillo,
el Dios que suda en la calle,
el Dios de rostro curtido.
You are the God of the poor,
the human and simple God,
the God who sweats in the street,
the God of the weather-beaten face.

Iraq was crowded with the faces of this God.
They watched as Sergeant Mejía said no to the other gods,
miniscule word, a pebble, a grain of rice,
but the word flipped that table at the war council,
where the bombardier god had just dealt
the last hand to the god of oil,
and cards with dates of birth and death,
like tiny tombstones, fluttered away.
Sergeant no more, Camilo Mejía walked to jail.
Commanders fed the word *coward*
to the sniffing microphones of reporters
who repeated obediently: *coward.*

The cell crowded with faces too, unseen travelers
wandering in from a century of jails:
union organizer, hunger striker, freedom rider,
street corner agitator, conscientious objector.

The God of the weather-beaten face,
dressed as an inmate steering a mop,
smuggled in the key one day, and Camilo Mejía
walked with him through epiphany's gate.

July 4, 2008   **Ed Sanders**

We gathered on the lawn
up the hill from
the oval of a pond
eating & talking
& celebrating our freedoms
The hosts had put
one of my poems,
in praise of "Goofitude"
in a frame by the food
It was a peaceful group
far from the missile-bearing drone-plane
or the suicide vests of no redemption
We WERE peace
o America!

peace on the lawn
in the hungry moments
of aging and attrition
peace in all its Peace!
& Time lay down its strictness
for a couple of hours
while we circled the lawn as surely
as our fellow beings the long yellow goldfish
in the pond below

Passive Resistance   **Enid Shomer**

Nevada Desert Experience

I'm teaching those who will step across the line to be arrested
that language can be violent, too, as yesterday, when they taunted
        the guide
on the government bus tour of the Nevada Nuclear Test
Site, blamed her for the puddled aluminum homes, the re-bar
        peeled

off the bank vaults like melted licorice sticks, the craters that
        look like the earth

sucked in its cheeks and held its breath. I've given them a "box of
        words"—
"neon," "casino," "angel"—to keep their righteousness from
        bursting forth.
I'm reading them my own bad lines to help them over the hurdle

of fear. But I came to Las Vegas with a secret motive—to drop a
        C-note
for my father, one year dead. I didn't attend the unveiling of his
        stone,
not wishing to show him respect, knowing that under his coat
of clay, he was still a threat, that his half-life decayed into mine.

Last night I clung to roulette as if to the helm of some ghost ship.
It took three hours to lose sixty bucks. I bet his birthday a dozen
times, won once and pulled ahead. The slot machines rolled ripe
cherries into my lap. My father adored, in the sense of
        worshipped, this cousin

to Disney World, with its waitresses dressed as slave girls,
        clockless rooms,
automatic change machines, Glitter Gulch's neon canyons.
Racing form, fishing dock or poker chips, he was always chumming
for luck. That is the gambler's lot—to live in the seconds *before*
        the dice run

aground on the felt or the racehorse pins the jockey's silks to the
        wind.
Now my students write faster under the plain-faced clock,
        cramming all
their passion into eight lines, using ten of the words which do not
        include
"justice," "bomb," "Nagasaki" or "atomic." Be personal,

I said—complicitous, not haughty. Imagine yourself on the
        wooden bleachers
happy to watch the desert lit from below by the incandescent
palsy of an underground bomb. Invent a science that could prosper
from 800 tests. Is evil a force or a lack, like the shadow that
        carves the crescent

moon? Tomorrow, they'll return to the Site, armed with hats, canteens
sunscreen and towels. They'll alert the police, tape their wrists
     for the handcuffs.
Tonight I'll lose the last forty dollars in a kind of mechanical
     keening,
playing the slots, craps, roulette again, games without a bluff.

I won't strew a bucket of chips on the floor to watch human
beings grovel, the way that my father would. I'll bet his
     birthday and deathday.
I'll lose without contempt for the gamblers, without resisting
     the odds, doom in
my emptying pockets as I near what must have been ground-zero

for him. I'll offer this peaceful protest against the violence he
     exacted
as his due. Let these be the last wages of Philip Steine.
Let them be clawed aside by the croupier, squandered like the
     origami
cranes folded in yesterday's seminar to nosedive onto the hottest
spot in the world while the disobedient cross the line.

Victory   Edwina Pendarvis

When a man, black like himself,
tried to grab his Olympic gold medal,

young Cassius Clay, soon to be Muhammad,
already the greatest,
fought him off easily,

then walked to the river
and slung the medallion far away, into the muddy
water.

He never felt stronger, he said.

My Test Market

Rachel Loden

Let's fly off to Finland, far
from the long arm of Olestra. There

in bog, arctic fen, and sand
are others who may understand

our epic innocence. Oh, how many
names for snow! and none

with growing market share. Where
are the snows that make no sense

so early in the morning, when the snow
is blue and blowing on the steppes?

Where is the *qanisqineq*,
the 'snow floating on water'?

We may ask Vigdís Finnbogadóttir,
who's not a Finn. She may not know,

but she may point us toward
the northern lights. Her aim is true,

her snowshoes always full of snow.
We won't come back. You come too.

Spring 1971 in Washington   Diane Kendig

The newspapers reported a "festive atmosphere,"
and many from my college had gone for the ride
that our only Poli Sci prof
had arranged to be educational.
We drove all night, marched all day, got one hour
for the Smithsonian, then boarded the bus
and drove all night back to Columbus.
Having come to understand for the first time
that I was going to die, not like Bob Roshong,
from my high school, who died in a border incursion,
but that I would one day be that irrevocably
not here, I was trying to stay awake
for the rest of my life, and I borrowed
a *Norton Anthology* to read while everyone slept,
and so found "The Mark on the Wall,"
which was not "The Yellow Wallpaper," I could see.
Most memories of that weekend
remain so crowded, crowded as the Mall,
where thousands had slept all night
and rose, mingled, and amassed,
so many people and buses, rarefied edges,
the way everything seems wavery
when you are young and haven't rested for weeks,
don't know where you are going,
waiting for something big that never comes—
except it did that second day,
not too long after sunset but in the dark,
before we got back on the bus,
nearing the Lincoln Memorial, lit up
with its columns, roped off: someone
I couldn't see at the edge of the portico played
a lone flute, a singular song that hung above
and after all, what stayed.

The People Who Pass By   (Oxford, 2003)   Lauren Rusk

They flow around us, our vigil a stone
in their stream, where High and Cornmarket
meet under an ancient clock.

One by one, we mostly can't be heard
protesting the first day of war
against Iraq. It's six PM, the light

lasting longer. Speakers' heads like horses'
shy away from the microphone.
I lean in to hear them say, we must

not kill. Students in turbans, gauze
tunics wafting, lean in too,
as each quarter hour drowns

a voice. Mechanical soldiers, Romans
freshly painted, hammer out the time.
And teenagers crouch on a doorstep, strumming

as if this were a festival. The river of people
surges on, accustomed to vigils, guitars,
mallets, and bells. What are they all doing

that's so important? Eating a bap.
Swinging a bag of fuchsia tissue paper
from the Oasis, some boutique.

Pulling a trolley of odds and ends,
perhaps to give the Oxfam shop. Or there,
leaning against the wall of that bakery,

breathing in. Shifting a headscarf, to cover
an errant tendril, or tilting a daughter's
pram up and over the curb;

apologizing, laughing, getting along;
quenching, lifting us, tumbling our edges,
the source, the wellspring, our unvoiced song.

The Fountain

Edward A. Dougherty

Three monks in yellow
outside the conference
against the death penalty
chanted *namyo myoho
renge kyo*, tapping
hand-drums, the beat
under everything that lives.
I remembered your letter
wishing "spring flowers
fill your days ahead
and may time for poetry
and gardening abound for you."
Tulips, some still hiding
their secret faces
in the day's bloom,
of themselves opened, heating
with heartwarmth
the dew-cool grass
and maroon stigma tips
of the pear flowers.
Like the moment monks
sang the morning's
inherent holiness, time
fills and overflows,
a fountain, a seed
eastering always
in blossom-time.

Maya Weiss Organizes
an Anti-War Rally in January 2007

Liane Ellison Norman

I really don't know why, she says.
A dozen kids make their own
posters to hold at the corner

of Forbes and Braddock
on a blustery day in the teens.
This corner's named for another

time, another war, when General
Braddock's forces failed to take
Fort Duquesne from General Forbes.

She's nearly seven, mover
and shaker: *My teacher's son
is in the war. Now he's in*

the hospital. Maybe, she thinks,
that's why. We're layered,
sweaters, parkas, hats, scarves,

mittens. More cars honk than
don't, thumbs up and the V
of first and second fingers,

the sign for peace. *Hey, Mr.
President. We're out here
in the cold saying No.*

Her Favorite Somali Fable Told to Her by Her Grandmother

Susan Rich

for Shukri Hassan

Arraweelo, peacekeeper
of men, queen
or saboteur, still
no one knows for sure.

What remains of Arraweelo
is her pleasure

in the swift kick

the forced removal of each soldier's
global genitals.

Arraweelo made a point
to have each man

promise to hold still
insisted, *the pain
it is not so bad...*

Honor required
she offer an award,
a chance for a man to return home
his private parts intact.

Perfumed with jasmine flowers
or fresh picked frankincense,

Arrawello lazed for hours
bathed as eight attendants
lathered up her arms,

a soft cloth for her neck,

her clavicle, her breasts,
until they arrived

between her ample legs.
And then she'd offer up
one man a golden comb

to gently clean between
each curl of pubic hair;
to take away the day's caked dust

and blood.
But most of all one rule:

his face could show no glimmer of disgust.

No turned down lip, no line
of commentary.

And if he concentrated
on just this task, could do his job
in a manner that pleased—

She'd know him as a humble man—

a man she'd trust to forget about fighting,
live with his neighbors in peace.

She'd send him home
with three young camels, sweet dates,
some Mogadishu tea.

Arraweelo, peacekeeper
of men, queen
or saboteur, still to this day,

who can say for sure
whether Arrawello's simple comb
might help us end the war.

Reincarnation of the Peace Sign   Jim Daniels

In 1972, my father-in-law, painting the flashing
on his roof, asked his daughter arriving home from school
what he should paint on the chimney.

He escaped Yugoslavia in 1960 without the language
to tell his war stories. He had an inexplicable love
for Mohammed Ali, and nostalgia for simple bread.

You could drive by that house and never notice
the red peace sign, but once it's pointed out
you'll never miss it again.

He was always on a high ladder, trying to color
the miracle of his own home. So quiet up there,
he once told his daughter it was safe to cross

the street, then a bike ran her down, broke her leg.
The world always exacting its slice
of cruelty. How could he have forgotten?

In 2004, he gives me permission to repaint peace.
My legs tremble on the 30-foot ladder. I try to trace
his old lines, but make a mess of it. Beneath me,

my children shout my name. I can barely hear them
in the rarified air. If you drive by now—*peace*,
a little brighter, a little harder to make out.

If you drive by now, honk your horn and wave.
The old man's getting a little deaf. His English
as good as it's going to get. He's inarticulate

with rage at the war's daily news.
But if you raise two fingers into a V
he will nod, and nearly smile.

Healing the Breach

Poems of Reconciliation

Christmas Soccer Game, 1915   Robert Cording

I suppose what made it possible
Was that no one expected more
Than a day of unhurried hours, better
Food, some free time to reread old letters,
Write new ones. Small Christmas trees
With candles lined both sides of the trenches
And marked the two days' truce.

Who can explain it?—one minute troops
Are sitting in mud, the next raising themselves
Out of the trenches, as if all they needed
Was a soccer ball to remind them
Of who they were. Imagine a Scotsman
Heading the ball into the air and catching it
On his instep, then flicking it across

The frosted grass to a German smoking
A cigarette who smiles and settles the ball,
Then boots it back. Soon a few soldiers
From both sides circle around the Scotsman
And the ball moves quickly back and forth,
Left foot, right foot, all of the men rocking
From side to side, the ball, the cold,

Making good neighbors of them all.
A game's begun, a real match without referees,
Attack and counterattacks, the ball crossing
From side to side, a match played,
We can imagine, as if it were all that mattered,
As if the game's sudden fizzes of beauty—
Three crisp passes or two perfect triangles

Lying end to end and pointing to the goal—
Could erase what they had learned
To live with. Laughing, out of breath, dizzy
With the speed of the ball skipping over
The frozen earth, did they recognize themselves
For a short while in each other? History says
Only that they exchanged chocolate and cigarettes,

Relaxed in the last ransomed sunlight.
When the night came and they had retreated
To their own sides, some of the men
Wrote about the soccer game as if they had to
Ensure the day had really happened. It did.
We have the letters, though none of them say
How, in the next short hours, they needed,

For their own well-being, to forget everything
That had happened that Christmas day.
It was cold, the long rows of candles must have
Seemed so small in the dark. Restless, awake
In the trenches, the men, I suppose,
Already knew what tomorrow would bring,
How it would be judged by the lost and missing.

Jerusalem   Naomi Shihab Nye

"Let's be the same wound if we must bleed.
Let's fight side by side, even if the enemy
is ourselves: I am yours, you are mine."
—Tommy Olofsson, Sweden

I'm not interested in
who suffered the most.
I'm interested in
people getting over it.

Once when my father was a boy
a stone hit him on the head.
Hair would never grow there.
Our fingers found the tender spot
and its riddles: the boy who has fallen
stands up. A bucket of pears
in his mother's doorway welcomes him home.
The pears are not crying.
Lately his friend who threw the stone
says he was aiming at a bird.
And my father starts growing wings.

Each carries a tender spot:
something our lives forgot to give us.
A man builds a house and says,
"I am native now."
A woman speaks to a tree in place
of her son. And olives come.
A child's poem says,
"I don't like wars,
they end up with monuments."
He's painting a bird with wings
wide enough to cover two roofs at once.

Why are we so monumentally slow?
Soldiers stalk a pharmacy:
big guns, little pills.
If you tilt your head just slightly
it's ridiculous.

There's a place in this brain
where hate won't grow.
I touch its riddles: wind and seeds.
Something pokes us as we sleep.

It's late but everything comes next.

On the Way Home   **Diane di Prima**
(A Prayer for the Road)

On the way home
all the restaurants will serve miso soup

On the way home
exotic notebook stores will blossom in small towns in Nevada

On the way home
Utah will be festooned w/mirth
Mormons will be dancing in the streets in gauzy *chatchkas*

On the way home
Everyone will leave the casinos and slot machines & go outside

to stare at the beauty of the mountains, of the sky, of each other

On the way home
All the boys & girls in the secret desert bordellos
will have set up temples of free love festooned with mimosa
they will teach karma-mudra to joyful redneck ranchers
who have set all their cows free and now drink only amrita

On the way home
every cafe in Wyoming will be holding a potlatch—
poverty will thus be abolished!

On the way home
everyone we meet will try to read us a poem
invite us in for a story   there being no news
but what travelers bring, all the TVs having died

On the way home
it will be easy to find pure water, organic tomatoes, friendly
                                                    conversation
We'll give & receive delightful music & blessings at every gas
                                                    station
(& all the gas will be free)

On the way home
all the truck drivers will drive politely
the traveling summer tourists will beam at their kids

our old Toyota will love going up mountain passes.
Openhearted & unsuspicious people & lizards
prairie dogs, wolves & magpies will sing together and picnic
at sunset beside the road

Everyone will get where they're going
Everyone will be peaceful
Everyone will like it when they get there

All obstacles smoothed
auspiciousness & pleasure
will sit like a raven dakini
on every roof

The Victory of Beit Jalla   Aharon Shabtai

"Realistic people for whom despair
feeds the devouring fire of hope"
-Eluard

A slap of the hand
will disperse the soldiers
like a swarm of flies.

The hills will bare
their well-scrubbed rears,
and the sun will polish the rooftops.

Eight-year-olds, ten-year-olds,
children aged eleven,
will emerge from their monastery lock-up.

Behind corners and under the beds,
they'll drop their stones
and, out in the alley,

one will gather his eye,
another the stump of his hand.

Into the back yard
our scarecrows' junk will be thrown.

In the village of Beit Jalla,
we'll fall in humility
onto the blackened necks
of our parents' parents—

here's the peasant
with the graying stubble
riding on the back of a donkey

wearing the glasses
with the cracked lens
of Joseph Posner!

We too will be refugees.
We'll sit shyly
at the edge of a blanket
spread out beneath the olive tree,
and, together,
eat hummus and a cucumber.

Lotem Abdel Shafi   Aharon Shabtai

The heart dies without space for love, without a moral horizon:
think of it then as a bird trapped in a box.
My heart goes out with love to those beyond the fence;
only toward them can one really advance, that is, make progress.
Without them I feel I'm half a person.
Romeo was born a Montague, and Juliet came from the Capulet
        line,
and I'm a disciple of Shakespeare, not Ben Gurion—
therefore I'll be delighted if my daughter marries the grandson of
        Haidar Abdel Shafi.
I mean this, of course, as a parable only—but the parable is my
        measure,
and since it has more to do with my body than teeth or hair,
this isn't just some idle fancy that, out of poetic license,
I place our fate in my daughter's sex.
That I grant myself this imaginary gift, testifies to the extent
to which we're living, still, in the underworld,
where we're granted the hope and potential of an amoeba.
But all mythology begins with creatures that creep and crawl,
spring out of the ground and devour each other,
until a sacred union occurs, healing the breach in the world.
The Arab groom from Gaza, too, will extend to my daughter a
        dress
on which is embroidered the Land redeemed from Apartheid's
        curse—
our Land as a whole, belonging equally to all of its offspring,
and then he'll lift the veil from her face, and say to her:
"And now I take you to be my wife, Lotem Abdel Shafi."

Uncle Charley

Allen Frost

I wonder what
he thought about
early morning
walking around
the big metal
bomber planes
before they flew

When did something
dawn on him
wake him up
and shine
on wings
like bolted
English dew

We Need a War

Mark Brazaitis

in which our soldiers, armed only
with heart-shaped canteens and humility,
invade the countries we deplore
with the deference and curiosity of third graders
on a field trip to see everything
they've ever been awed by.
We'll count as wounded the soldiers
who become so enchanted with the languages
of these detested countries,
they speak them as if each word began
a poem.
We'll count as mortally wounded the soldiers
who find in the sunsets of these despicable lands
enough of the pinks and oranges they've known
all their lives to say, "I could be home,"
and, in their next breath,
understand they are.
And our missing? They will be the soldiers who disappear
with this strange man, or that woman from the shadows,

go AWOL in the swamps and sands of attraction
only to emerge camouflaged by love,
which will make even the most martial of them
glow like gardeners in a blooming garden.
We need a war that begins with a victory parade
in which we shower our enemies with confetti
in the colors and shapes of what we all hold sacred.
Afterwards, we'll hand them microphones,
and when they're finished saying
what we need to hear, we will, together,
compose a treaty made of music,
something reverent yet danceable,
something even the most unmusical of us can hum,
something that might sound, in places and to hopeful ears,
like the preflight rustling of a bird's feathers.
A dove's, perhaps. Of course, a dove's.

Teacups in the Air   Gail Hosking Gilberg

It's not the best china, not worth
a great battle, but still
its breaking toasts an unsettling song
as we go over, *I said, you said*:
stories we can both believe.

I weep for honesty, want it poured
in my cup like the nectar the hummingbird
takes at the porch's edge. I'll add
a plate of cookies for humor, some warm milk
to bring you before bed, the same cup

I caught midair just before
it hit the tiled floor. I admire
the delicacy of the cup's floral pattern,
the way we save it for future fights,
the strength of porcelain.

Making Peace in Jerusalem   Joanne Seltzer

Across the valley
from the Western Wall
my husband and I sit
under a gnarled olive tree.

Feathery leaves conceal
the unripe remnant
of last year's crop
but I find an olive, pick it,
roll it in the palm of my hand
then cast it to the ground,
a single die
in the survival game.

Veterans of the marriage wars
we share four children,
knapsack heavy with bad years,
a taste for briny olives,
domesticities.

At the State Correctional Facility   Emily K. Bright

"We're going to find words," they tell Security
as I lead the English class of ten, minus one locked-down
today, outside to observe the trees. Write down everything
you can, I say, and they go at it eagerly, not questioning,
perhaps, the odd ways of a poet. Plus there's sun and
breeze today, we're at the center of this green campus;
we can't see the fences from here. The kid with THUG
LOVE on his knuckles says his tree is *cozy*. All those shabby
leaves like *fur*. We find *loser* trees and *confused* trees.
A patrolling car on route stops by to say hello. There are
things far worse than winding up at *juvy*. Like possibly, not
stepping out, not coming here at all. The ash the class has
gathered round is "dull—not climbable," says THUG LOVE.
We count the limbs sliced off, we puzzle at its cinched-in base,
chipped by the careless mower. All these guys have been addicted,
who knows who has been abused or what they have inflicted.

They sit on the grass, all uniforms and sculpted faces,
not "fixed" and attentive. About the ash, the boy with doll eyes
says, "It looks like the kid that just takes it and takes it silently
until one day it snaps." Scared to read them poetry, I stall
until there's time for just one, then read to them of ocean.
All nine listen, eyes fixed, still: young men who see everything,
who see, who want to look.

Cease Fire: Batticaloa, Sri Lanka   Marilyn Krysl

The war had turned inward until it resembled
suicide. The only soothing thing was water.
I passed the sentries, followed surf out of sight.
I would sink into the elements, become simple.

Surf sounds like erasure, over and over.
I lay down and let go, the way you trust an animal.
When I opened my eyes, all down the strand
small crabs, the bright yellow of a crayon,

had come out onto the sand. Their numbers, scattered,
resembled the galactic spill and volume of the stars.
I, who had lain down alone, emptied,
waked at the center of ten thousand prayers.

Who would refuse such attention. I let it sweeten me
back into the universe. I was alive, in the midst
of great loving, which is all I've ever wanted.
The soldiers of both sides probably wanted just this.

Consanguinity   Tom Kryss

In a book about canal locks, I find the perfect description
of how memory works. My favorite description of the heart
is one in which the writer on the face of it seems to be examining
leather hinges and hidden spaces of an old seaman's trunk.
It's uncanny and wonderful how they do this.
                    They may not even know they are doing it.
Like the change of heart which brings peace simply because
inside it is broken, mirroring the world. A dead tree in a field
to which birds fly for no discernible benefit. Grass which grows
in rusted cans by the tracks. Old barns falling back into earth,
so crazily tilted it's the tilting which holds them together:
underpinnings of peace. Gears of peace: hydraulic processes,
tropisms, mountain building. Eye of peace: sea glass. You.

Dag Hammarskjöld: Tom Kryss

I broke up a fight this past summer
at the edge of the concrete court.
One of the boys had come running to me—
to me!—for protection, he hid at my back,
still screaming and carrying on,
and attached himself to my legs; then
the other ran up, fists clenched,
and lunged circles around me,
trying to get his hands around the throat
of the smaller kid who, maintaining
a steady barrage of recrimination
and taunts, never let go and kept circling,
bobbing, ducking, it was giving me
a severe case of the vertigo. I said, "Stop it!
I don't care which of you started this—
I don't wish to see it again!" Immediately—
or as immediately as could be arranged—
the combatants froze just long enough
to notice something—perhaps a mutual
underlying interest—and walked off together,
practically side by side, discussing what was left

of the matter in quiet, serious tones.
I don't know how I did it—it surprised even me.
Months later the death toll count hits
for the one thousandth time in ways
that only it can. Still favoring my lower back,
I limp off the plane at the airstrip in the Democratic
Republic of Congo, and open the briefcase:
it is empty. I must have left the statement
in Stockholm. They are waiting to hear
something, and they are all holding guns.
I know these are the heights of naivete. *What,*
at this point, would be the harm in a little naivete?
Enough. Stop, I say. Then, I am swarmed
by an escort, and hurried into a jeep.

A Story of War   Larry Smith

My grandson and I visit the history museum.
He is six and always asking, so we
tour the cases, a war for each one,
beginning with 1812, fought off-shore on Lake Erie.
But what has drawn him into history's web
is the Civil War, book images of men
in a field wielding swords and bayonets
and long rifles—"How many inches, Grandpa?"

I am a pacifist, a veteran of no wars,
yet I walk with him and his questions.

Two days ago we strolled the Confederate Cemetery
on Johnson's Island, where men locked up men
and buried those who could not survive.
And what is left are head stones and small Rebel flags,
a tall statue of one with his long gun—
put up by the Daughters of the Confederacy.

A young boy and an old man among headstones,
I try to explain to him and myself
the reasons for that war and others.
And he looks up at me in mid-sentence, in that

field of graves and says, "Grandpa, I would not
risk my life to kill another person"—That simple
and true to his own innocence. I tell him
I honor their bravery but not their killing.
"Right," he says, and we let that moment stand
as our being together on a battleground.

We trade the museum for lunch in a diner.
Over milkshakes and burgers, he says,
"Grandpa, I love the war." And I, "You do?"
"Not the killing. Not that, but your stories
of the battlefields." I somehow know
and let it stand, a truth between us.

Silent on the long drive home,
I turn to say, "I love you, Adam, and
I am not going to die for a long time."
And he answers back, "Never."

You Have the Right to a Cessation of Hostilities

Naton Leslie

The night would draw down over us, and iron anger
would sear after my father's shift at the mill.

I could hear his car arrive beside the house,
the sputtering carburetor troubling my spine.

He would enter and slam. He would stomp and demand.
My mother would send out emissaries of excuses.

I was short. I was thin. I had not done the chores.
I was nervous, distracted. How could I be his son?

But he shrank as I grew older, and I forgave him.
I let him retract his temper, reinvent a good man.

I remained his son. I stopped balling my fists
under the blankets. I stopped being the pain.

The crows left the trees in exaltation. The deer
made their dances. The raccoons formed a league.

The geese spelled the way out. Dogs sang in harmony.
All the tomatoes ripened. The sky removed its mask.

A woman kissed me back. The leaves stayed on the trees.
My eyes ceased to narrow. I no longer need aspirin.

My father asked me to understand, to recognize a treaty.
I have paid for my peace. I cannot be Montressor.

I hope you too can survive. I believe there are balms.
May you get through the dark with dim lights.

Drink up my friend. Be lighter than your reasons,
faster than your past, and slower than the love of others.

The Program   Rosaly DeMaios Roffman

Mother Theresa says when asked
how she does it, "Come see"
as she strokes the face of a twitching child
until the convulsions stop

and it is this image that we carry forth
of a great fish out of the water,
the gone perfume carrying on with gone colors
every mere child under mercy

and the sway of this imperative
springs forth like a flower breaking under water,
the politics of ordinary men and language
not up to the gesture of seeing but catching on

These lives become, like biography,
not so important, like the image
of that fish out of water, transparent;
the passion of belief could save us

if everywhere we could hear the sounding
of the broken body of a child—and
watch someone like this mother stumble
through the boundaries of desert to save us

whether we, past rubble and medals,
believe in reasons to be saved or not

Shock and Awe   **Mike Schneider**

March 19, 2003, bombs fall on Baghdad

Old Mister Gramley across the street
          has a white husky with a twisted leg
and evil eye. She yowls to heaven.
          Such grief. As if everything is sour

as the green moon in a black sky.
     His big house with a broken doorbell
is like my government, too many
          broken doorbells to count. Too many

windows of thick glass, well insulated
     people in dark suits with ties that shine,
faces that smile the greasy, crooked smile
          that means Damn, our bombs are smart,

aren't they? While a snare drum rattles
     and Earth opens for business. These people.
If only they could howl their incandescent
          lies like dogs in heat until their tongues

droop. If only they were yappy circus dogs
                    in a slapstick movie. We'd laugh
at the sight of their dogmatic minds clamped
          like jaws on a frayed rope. They tug and tug,

possessed puppies twisting their heads until
          with a growl the madness lets go. Their lonely

ideas lift in the sky like bright balloons.
        Don't worry. They won't fall on your house

or mine. As this imagined movie arrives
        at its happy end, so different from life,
we turn to each other, hold hands
        and stroll into the evening, the sidewalk

solid beneath us. And I remember dodge ball
        with Peggy Smith, who was beautiful
in second grade. I remember when I had
        no idea of the things I didn't know.

The Daily Contortions   Philip Metres

He's rushing down the block, away
from *shul*, dressed in black hat, black
coat and pants, even black socks
peeking beneath lemon yellow

crocs. *Yom Kippur*—my daughter's
ten-year-old friend Tehila informs us—
you can't wear leather, you don't eat,
you get the chance to become

an angel. The kids are gathered, chosen
neighbors around Aviva's swing,
whose arc's so wide you wonder
if you're flying. The seat chains ascend

to a limb so high it's heaven,
whatever our religion. We take turns
giving underdogs, which means helping
others to *wing*, as Leila says,

still lacking letters. Who can use
the swing, what symbols printed
on boxes indicate something is
not forbidden—these are the daily

signs we study and are
flummoxed by. In the meantime,
Aviva, our neighbor, the splitting
image of my daughter, refuses

her pretzels: *I don't give non-Jews
pretzels*, she explains, then,
*but I can give them to my dog.
But Adele's almost Jewish*, Rahel

insists. *Aren't you, Adele?*
Who among us does not want *pretiola*—
"little rewards" the monks would grant
to children reciting Bible verses,

which, read wrongly, one day would darken
into *Kristallnact*? The little arms
of *bracchia* folded in prayer, a crucifixion
treat to savor and swallow. Here, the daily

contortions continue. Who can do
what and who cannot and by what
law is it possible, and to sate
which God hungry for our obedience?

I want to shake this little angel,
the flaming sword of her words
expelling my daughter
from the garden

of her sunburned yard. The peace process
is a matter of a third girl, Rahel,
breaking her pretzel,
handing the savory splinter to Adele.

The Folly of Half

Sarah Zale

Aman understands the walnut,
how the line of its equator,

like pressed lips, waits.
She understands the avocado,

sliced from point to round,
how one half falls away

from the pit. She misses it.
She is Muslim-Arab, she is

Israeli. She is two mismatched
socks, alone, after all the clothes

are folded. Solomon understands
the folly of splitting the baby.

So it says in Kings 3, in the Qur'an.
Aman is waiting for her mother

to cry out. My ear drops
to the belly of the land. I am

listening. Something stirs.
I feel it kick.

The Point We Meet   Elmaz Abinader

On Christmas day, my father teaches his granddaughter
to crack walnuts with her bare hands. He gathers two in his fist,
their bark scraping against his palm. His fingers are long
and old country elegant, bronze, manicured and strong.
When he flexes his palm, the nuts divide, opening
cleanly as lemons, the flesh intact in the heart.

His granddaughter cannot believe she can do this,
hands so small, loose as cattails. *Use both* he prompts,
meaning her hands and chooses two walnuts for her,
almost identical in size. She clasps her fingers
together and presses, her shoulders rise,
her neck stretches; the veins on the back of her hand
fill with blood.

Her palms, open,
blush with failure, the two nuts rolling
against each other. My father reaches over and turns them,
tells her, *try again*. He nods confident, flicks a finger forward.
She is that kind of girl, one who holds worlds inside her hands,
one who will push. When the nuts meet, this time, everything
gives in–their crack is scientific, the dissection, a neat surgery.

They lie open on the coffee table, unwhole, yet not broken.
My father picks out the meat, *it doesn't take strength*, he says.
He draws a circle around them, where the two halves come
together, it's where they are weak. Position them
at their points of vulnerability.

His granddaughter rejoices, runs to show her brother
her new trick. I take one walnut, rattled it beside my ear,
I have been deceived by the stubbornness of the shell,
the strength of the construction, stronger than teeth.
We crushed them with rocks and hammers, lining them up
on the porch after they fell from the tree, shed
their green crisp coat, ready to be eaten. They did not
split as they gave way to our instruments, exposing
the compartments of their interior. Crushing mixed
the inside and the outside into heaps of crumbs.

We were scavengers, picking out flesh from bone,
satisfied with getting in, anyway we could.

Is it too much to say, there is finer humanity
in breaking walnuts by hand? Is it too false
to find lines of connection, seams of conjunction,
and push against them, ever so slightly? The simplicity
of this is trustworthy—too classical to borrow from.
When tenderness aligns, everything opens without the sloppiness
of destruction or residue of incompetence.

I think of the forces I can push with my hands:
silence against loneliness, peace against solace,
the tremble of love against whispers at dusk.
So much is offered to us that
simultaneously erupts
as we touch it ever so gently.
A walker who is lost
in a wood that is patient.
A dream that lives inside the memory
of a woman dying on her damp couch.
The fineness of a young girl on Christmas
sitting with her grandfather seeking
what is held in his hands. I put my palms
together to rub what is hidden there
that I can press into becoming something edible
useful. Nothing emerges, but each word
that is uttered at the heat of creation.

Twigs   Taha Muhammad Ali

Neither music,
fame, nor wealth,
not even poetry itself,
could provide consolation
for life's brevity,
or the fact that *King Lear*
is a mere eighty pages long and comes to an end,
and for the thought that one might suffer greatly
on account of a rebellious child.

*

My love for you
is what's magnificent,
but I, you, and the others,
most likely,
are ordinary people.

*

My poem
goes beyond poetry
because you
exist
beyond the realm of women.

*

And so
it has taken me
all of sixty years
to understand
that water is the finest drink,
and bread the most delicious food,
and that art is worthless
unless it plants
a measure of splendor in people's hearts.

*

After we die,
and the weary heart
has lowered its final eyelid

on all that we've done,
and on all that we've longed for,
on all that we've dreamt of,
all we've desired
or felt,
hate will be
the first thing
to putrefy
within us.

Savoring the World

Poems of Shared Humanity

From "This Connection of Everyone With Lungs" — Juliana Spahr

December 4, 2002

Embedded deep in our cells is ourselves and everyone else.

Going back generations we have nine thousand ancestors and going back twenty-five we get thirty million.

All of us shaped by all of us and then other things as well, other things such as the flora and fauna and all the other things as well.

When I speak of yours thighs and their long muscles of smoothness, I speak of yours cells and I speak of the British Embassy being closed in Kenya and the US urging more aggressive Iraq inspections and the bushfire that is destroying homes in Sydney.

And I speak of at least one dead after rioting in Dili and the arrest of Mukhlas, and Sharon's offer of 40 percent of the West Bank and the mixed results of Venezuela's oil strike and the overtures that Khatami is making to the US.

When I speak of the curve of yours cheeks, their soft down, their cell after cell, their smoothness, their even color, I speak of the NASA launch and the child Net safety law and the Native Linux pSeries Server.

When I speak of our time together, I speak also of the new theories of the development of the cell from iron sulfide, formed at the bottom of the oceans.

I speak of the weight of the alien planet.

And I speak of the benefits of swaddling sleeping babies.

Beloveds, all our theories and generations came together today in order to find the optimum way of lacing shoes. The bow tie pattern is the most efficient.

I want to tie everything up when I speak of yous.

I want to tie it all up and tie up the world in an attempt to understand the swirls and patterns.

But there is no efficient way.

The news refreshes every few minutes on the computer screen and on the television screen. The stories move from front to back and then off the page and then perhaps forward again in a motion that I can't predict but I suspect is not telling the necessary truths.

I can't predict our time together either. Or why we like each other like we do.

I have no idea when our bodies will feel very good to one of us or to all of us together or to none of us.

The drive to press against one another that is there at moments and then gone at others.

The drive to press up against others in the same way.

[*Double plural of "yours" and "yous" is deliberate.]

The Road to Rama   Sam Hamill

Where is the road to Rama
and how far can I go alone?

Here is the road to Rama, friend,
here in the dust of our bones.

And here is the house of an Arab
with its sleepy summer garden,
its olive tree and its shade.

You count the bullet holes, my friend,
and fill its empty craters,
but you cannot number the dead.

And here is the house of a Jew—
and the strangest thing—
it looks exactly the same:

the same garden, same olive tree,
same craters in the garden,
same bloodstains in the sand.

Here on the road to Rama
I hope to find my brother,
the poet Samih Al-Qasim,

before it is too late.
I have wandered far in the desert,
thirsting for his words.

Have you heard my brother, the poet?
He will break your heart and mend it
with the sadness of his song.

Have you seen my brother, the poet?
I am weary of smoke and dust,
and the road is long, and I am growing old.

I will die on the road to Rama,
my heart cradled by his song.

Beach Road, Beirut to Miramar Resort
Susan Azar Porterfield

My driver may have been Hezbollah—
hard to say,
a young man, serious in that way
some young men here are.

They walk without unraveling,
keeping their eyes below ground. They wait.
For work, for women.
They wait and flare and are not light.

Even his smile, when it came,
tied in as an alien ship.
He understood the way to survive
meant more of my kind

arriving everyday.
It's possible he was Hezbollah.
In how he talked—justice, Iraq,
and the ones who sacrifice lives.

Why, he asked, did America,
rigid spine of human rights, just
shrug at Palestinian hurt? *You must not*

drink the water, he advised and stopped
so I could buy three liters-full.
You will need food.
And he stopped again, then unasked,

hauled my suitcases, the burden
of my being, water and groceries
upstairs. He placed them just inside
the door. *You will like it here.*

Open the curtains, he said.
The dark room exploded
in sea-light and a cooling breeze, and yes,
I think, perhaps, he was Hezbollah.

Make-Up Lessons

Susan Azar Porterfield

(University of Balamand, Lebanon)

At the blackboard, I'm rumpled and dun.
To inspire beauty and truth, I ask my students,

must art be beautiful and true?
In the first row, all term, Raja's tried to teach me

the art of maquillage. She's kind and concerned
and after class, suggests a special facial cream,

how to rim my eyes with kohl.
I'm the shabby American, who is also Lebanese,

a woman of the tribe. It's what she'd council
a favored aunt, it's mother-to-daughter advice.

Beauty is intimate, she instructs, and pushes me
to pluck my brows blank and write them in clean,

reality and truth are lovers, not friends.
I'm the rhyme she's trying to revise, doggerel

to designer, since poetry, I've lectured,
can make us finer, more alive.

It's a lesson she seems to get,
in her way, and I'm grateful she sees me

worthy of a luminous cheek. *It's about light*,
I tell my class. It can tart up the plainest poem.

Savoring The World   Dane Cervine

Washington DC, a warm evening in November,
sitting outside the Sultan's Palace waiting for a gyro,
sipping Almaza beer while the world rolls by,
students from Georgetown & Howard universities
chattering on cell phones, and I have never been so happy
to be alone, listening, open as a gate in this corner chair,
the sensory soup of neighborhood, globe,
anywhere I look *seeing* what God was aiming at,
the words *ordinary, mundane* made up later
by those with a short attention span. *Look!*
at the silver sport utility vehicle gliding by,
windows rolled down, blaring bass syncopating
with the sirens searing down the adjacent block:
could it get any better than *this!* And the faces
of Arab, African, & Asian so at ease you could almost believe
the Shoe Repair sign across the street:
that anything broken can be mended here.

And so I listen to the bald man in white shirt,
white slacks, white shoes tell his cell phone
my brother died of AIDS ten years ago, and I'm still grieving.
And how the jaunty-capped black man lights up
with *Mother!* as his cell phone jingles, flips open,
carries the voice of the one he loves. Listen
to how the world can only be what it is—
invoke the sirens circling now like dogs
to keep at bay the rabid snarl of wanting things
to be other than they are. Like the blond woman
in the crosswalk just now, two Dobermans leashed
& serene: there's no fathoming what goes on inside,
the political science of hormone & heart begging détente,
a kind of soul you could actually live in.

So when my gyro comes—all tactile & aroma—
every taste bud kneels down, prays
that this pepper mixed with sweet bean,
this flesh of fowl & wheat, be its own sacrament—
savoring the carnal world sacred.

Somewhere   Joan E. Bauer

you open a newspaper & wonder if atoms in
your fingers as they tap at the newsprint can be felt

on the sub-atomic scale in Darfur, where haggard men
in sweaty t-shirts grunt as they unload sorghum seed, soap,

powdered milk. They do not worry about the sub-atomic scale.
Only if, after drought, the rains will come

& if those are dust clouds in the distance
                              & to whom should one pray?

Somewhere, a surgeon removes an obstinate shard of shrapnel.
The gods permit this. Somewhere a mute old woman

(with begging bowl & tick welts the size of a dime)
sits in the shade of palms. Soldiers

lounge in stupor at the edge of the mud-walled village.
Women cook doura & bean cakes.

Hanoi, 1996   Joan E. Bauer

God save us always from the innocent and the good.
— Graham Greene, The Quiet American

The airport, a strife-worn shell, encroached by green.
Flood fields of rice, water buffalo. I am alone,

but for those guards. Coarse uniforms, red stars.
Soldiers or police? I don't ask. Young boys approach

to sell their thin-paged books. "You are Chinese?"
(My Cherokee eyes miscast me everywhere)

"In school we study English every day!" Dusty bus ride
to the City of Lakes. Shift-streams of jeeps, old bikes,

tri-shaws. Red banners skitter. A huge and smiling
Ho Chi Minh, dove and child. By late-day light, I criss-

cross bustling streets that bloom with brass-caged birds,
hand-painted screens. Aged to ochre, the French facades.

In Hoan Kiem, I find a glistening lake. Yellow blossoms
frame the view: a crimson bridge, legs like lanky cranes.

At dusk, I see pagodas melt to grey. Two frail, white-
bearded men, silent on a bench. "Not one angry glance,"

I whisper to the sky. "They won, so now they *like* you,"
sky replies. "The sin of pride was yours, don't you agree?"

By night, the city swells with steaming pots. A street-side
feast of *pho,* with clams and eel. An ancient *grandmere*

shakes her head and smiles, "You have no children?
Sad! So sad!" Sidewalk smoke floats past the flowers.

I see four generations gathered. I know beyond banners,
smiles, facades—despair. Soldier's twisted limbs,

hovels built of tin, cheap wood. A hundred years of conflict.
They survived. Beneath the Hanoi moon, I saw it there.

Carolyn Forché's in El Salvador — Vivian Shipley

but I'm next in line at the Dixwell Stop and Shop.
Artichokes, strawberries, asparagus, turkey
for economy, I figure up the total and count bills
to speed up my check out, but the woman in front
of me sorts out coins. I'm impatient, even though
I can see she's old with a hole in her sweater
big enough for me to stuff my fist through.
Leave enough for bus fare, the checkout clerk
urges. The light bulbs are left behind. I buy the pack,
knowing it's like dropping money in the collection
plate at church, but I feel good as the bagger gives me
an approving look. I rush from the store just as
she boards the bus, bringing no light, bridging no gulf.

Declaration of War — Marilyn Krysl

Midnight. The equator. Stillness
like a mirror. Here nothing

is easy, and the soldiers edgy.
Beside the bridge, a sentry

leans against a bunker. The road
mined. Rice fields, green satin,

and beyond, the sea: that constant
inconstancy. I get up, go out,

stand on a slab of moonlight. Water
lapping bruised sand. Soldier,

lover, whoever comes—if the leper,
if the torturer—wash the feet

of that stranger. In my pocket
is one glove. You have the other.

The Sacrosanct   Gerry LaFemina

In Manhattan again, in the midst of midtown businessmen
& women with briefcases & designer sunglasses
I stop at D'agostino's where I buy two apples,
two blood oranges & two apricots. I am not
hungry. There's the R train downtown
to Canal Street, Chinatown's sulfurous tip.
I walk East & South in blocks
to find this place I've been many times
before; as always I bow to the Buddha
& to the old woman who sweeps the floor
& to the monk's creased bald head.
He is a walking wick, aglow, in his silence.
I place two apricots, two oranges &
an apple before the statue. There's enough fruit here
already—grapefruits bigger than my fists, mangos,
bananas. & what of my other apple?
I gave it to the rag man bound for Brooklyn.
How he eyed the fruit suspiciously, holding it
up to the artificial light for sixty long seconds
till finally he bit into it with a spray of sweet juices
that christened his chin, golden in that yellow glow.
Mmm delicious, he said, *delicious* like a mantra;
rocking southbound, seventy feet beneath those streets.

For Giving   Dora McQuaid

> *For the participants of the Impact of Violence Program at the*
> *Pennsylvania State Correctional Institution for Men at Houtzdale,*
> *and for Dawn McKee.*

They write me letters.
Their 4th grade handwriting,
the paper scored by pen and pencil indent
from the force and focus of their intention.
Often on blue-lined, loose-leaf paper;
occasionally on colored construction paper;
sometimes on coloring-book pages mounted

to the colored-paper, and then folded,
like the greeting cards I made at age 8,
with the Crayola 24-pack with its back-box sharpener.

When I unfold the pages, their breath reaches up
to me as though captured while they held it,
through the crafting and the writing.
I think always of their hands,
the length of fingers,
the scoring of lines and scars on palm and finger face,
the thickness of their wrists,
the hollowness in the cups of them when they are at rest.
And then of the capacity of these same hands,
these hands that write me letters,
that craft cards for me,
for rage, for violence, for annihilation.

One reading I did, I was edgy and scared before them.
I felt on the wrong side of the door again.
There was no screaming this time,
no blood temple hovering,
no chest beating menace in the vicinity of my heart.
But, I was behind the barbs again,
3 layers of it rolled above the chain-link and the trips
and the vastness of the open fields beyond the barriers.

My eyes kept returning to the crows in those fields,
above the eyes and heads of those men,
above their hands,
which I could barely stop watching,
barely escape vigilance of their positioning,
of their foretelling.
I was watching breathing patterns, too, and
muscle twitches, waiting for the spring
toward me as I read poems of my blood father's wrath
and my lover's rage
and my spirit caving like an animal gone to ground,
curling around the wounding
before learning to rise again,
enough to do all of this telling.

The crows gave me comfort,
their wheel and loft.
Their raucousness reminded me:
I leave here soon.
I needed reminder that escape, again,
was a possibility.
I told myself the crows will carry me
until I can cross the barbs again
and let sleep find me,
while Dawn drives us away,
outside, safely, together.

When I did look up from the poem into the hour,
afraid of the hands of the man in front of me,
at the end of his 6-foot, 5-inch frame,
that had wrung out the life of a woman,
those hands were steepled before him.
He was hiding the crying,
but I could see it.
I met his eyes, finally.
He lowered his hands.
We cried together, while the room of men,
dressed in Department of Corrections mauve-issue
hung on, around us.

Silent then, I left.
I dreamt of him behind the barriers.
He wrote to me, shared a poem
and his own dark history behind its making.
He ended the letter with:
God bless you.
The indentation in the paper on those words was a ripple.
And on the words:
You saved me. I am grateful.
I rubbed my finger over the ridge he'd made with the giving.

His hands made this bridge from there to me,
as my voice made the bridge from here to him.
And this is how we save each other:
With our hands and the breath between us.

Something Like a Sonnet for Something Like Peace

Jim Daniels

Pittsburgh, 2003

In high school, I lusted after the jagged cruelty of spray paint,
    anonymous
slander of the foreign. Today, I lust after Salaam's meats sizzling
    on the grill
chained to the fence outside his tiny grocery store. For a morsel
    dropped
from Salaam's tongs into my open hands, I offer up my stopped
    wristwatch

and a pack of matches from my brother's first wedding in 1975
    after Nixon
abolished the draft. If God exists, would he want capital letters?
    Would he
let anyone stumbling or strutting down the streets of this broken
    city
determine his will, steal this grill? Today I abandon the smudged
    newsprint

of blood and the gnashing curses muted into polite musings. I
    once lusted
after somebody else's prayers. I remain in fear's limbo. Today I'm
    chewing
the holy meat on the street in September sun, juice running down
    my chin.
I share a silent nod with Salaam. Above the clicking of meters
    counting out

greed, above the cacophonic brass of cars on the boulevard,
I hear the wind chimes of the neighborhood stutterer.

Res Publica   Anna Meek

Nothing so intimate as this: the insane woman
is shouting, starting out on her walk.
Her mind is at war. Her voices draft us from sleep

to join each other in the street. Neighbors
cluster around her like bees. In the open,
danger resembles a plate of honey. We find our body
sweet, and ominous. Perhaps we cannot help ourselves.
Perhaps we are touching

our homeland, O homeland, delicious curves,
rosehips, shored wet edges; it stretches our naked
and implicated privacies. Transgression, invasion:
we cannot steal ourselves from one another.

The Way We Learn to Love the World

Poems of Nature & Home

The Peace of Wild Things   Wendell Berry

When despair grows in me
and I wake in the middle of the night at the least sound
in fear of what my life and my children's lives may be,
I go and lie down where the wood drake
rests in his beauty on the water,
and the great heron feeds. I come into the peace of wild things
who do not tax their lives with forethought
of grief. I come into the presence of still water.
And I feel above me the day-blind stars
waiting with their light. For a time
I rest in the grace of the world, and am free.

Trying to Understand the Patriot Act   Todd Davis

Where I've been pulling stone from the edge
of the field, a mother killdeer screams at me.
She tries desperately to get my attention, pretends

her right wing is broken, letting it flop like a flag
at half-mast. Her nest must be near, but I don't see it,
nor hear the young she seeks to protect. When I come

too close to turn over a stone, judge its weight,
decide whether I can lift it into the bed of the truck,
she flies hard, up and away, banking, then drawing

a perfect circle across the field, showing me
the shape of air in the presence of fear.

Optimism   Jane Hirshfield

More and more I have come to admire resilience.
Not the simple resistance of a pillow, whose foam
returns over and over to the same shape, but the sinuous
tenacity of a tree: finding the light newly blocked on one side,
it turns in another. A blind intelligence, true.
But out of such persistence arose turtles, rivers,
mitochondria, figs—all this resinous, unretractable earth.

February Report on Conditions   Jeff Gundy
in the Interior

1. I was either too early or too late again this morning, but the
    sun had me covered.
2. The tips of Scotch pine littering the back yard have stayed
    green for weeks. I still don't know if the wind or some
    demented squirrel took them down.
3. Last night the neighbor on the corner drove her old Buick up
    over the curb and parked on her own grass again.
4. Last week in Samarra, our guys drove their Humvee back to
    base with two dead insurgents strapped to the hood like
    deer.
5. The square of plywood nailed over the bottom half of the
    lime-green garage's broken window years ago is holding.
6. The three strange angels have not been seen in weeks.
7. No snow since December, and the ice-shelves along the
    creekbank are shrinking and cracking.
8. Agonizing reappraisals of the true, the good, and the right
    continue.
9. Somebody sawed the big fallen limb into lengths just right
    for burning, then left them on the brown grass like a puzzle
    for dummies.
10. Everybody I know still showers completely naked. As far as I
    know.
11. *There is no one sleeping*, wrote Tony Hoagland.
12. I met him once in a diner in Baltimore, which is nowhere
    near Samarra.
13. *There is no one sleeping,* he wrote, *who does not dream of
    being touched.*

14. The leftover bale of straw is still at the edge of the garden, slowly and irreversibly becoming something else.
15. *A crucial dimension is one of humility,* wrote my smart friend.
16. *The gospels can be read as an anamnesis of blindness,* wrote his smart friend.
17. The president is threatening veto, but his minions are still restless.
18. The skaters are beautiful, strong, and angry.
19. Death said, "I was surprised to see your servant here in Baghdad, for tonight I must meet him in Samarra."
20. My eyes feel better since I've been using the lotion.
21. I can't lose those three Christmas pounds, though I've been riding the cursed bike every night.
22. Maybe tomorrow my heart will break out, or open, or down.
23. Maybe two riders are approaching and the wind will begin to howl.
24. Maybe my soul will grow so slender it can slip between sash and frame and enter the seamless blue.
25. A great golden dome was shattered yesterday in Samarra.
26. *Want to live forever?* the email asks, but the message is empty.
27. Tonight we start to build another dome, in the secret place where the gospel is always clear and silent.
28. The ducks are still on the pond.

Firefly   Jeff Gundy

I want to find the room where my father is sleeping
take his hand and wake him. I will say I am sorry

to have come so late, after all the other children.
I will ask about his heart and his dreams,

apologize for disturbing his rest. I want to drive there
faster than anybody, but I am not even on the way home.

The masters say all is one, but I am five hundred miles away,
studying the alphabet of broken trees

and the gorgeous dusk of the beaver marsh.
The masters say nothing is separate, but I am lost

among the lilies, the needly mosquitoes, the slow tenderness
of the fireflies. I will leave tomorrow if need be.

Tonight I will dream of the great healing,
and the night will be warm with the hum of fireflies,

the chir and splish of the beavers fitting one more stick,
one more slap of mud in the mile-long dam.

And there's plenty to be unhappy about   Rosemerry Wahtola Trommer

but first, I think I will run through dry leaves
at the park with my boy, roll down hills
like we're drunken logs, spin on the merry go round
till our stomachs spiral and lurch into *stop*.

Seems to me, and I'm thankful, that skepticism
makes a lousy scarf to warm the neck. Better
to gather this pre-winter sun into memory swatches.
Warmth comes when we play, run through dry grass
like white seeds in wind gusts, pretend we are kites.

The seed and dry leaf resemble each other,
both fly toward reinvention. The bird flies
otherwise, has a wingspan for intention. And we?
The day is barren, yes. And brittle. Comes cold
from the turning, the turning without.

Brown friend, the lively sparrow rises
like comedy from the pile of leaves
and hops along the naked tree.
In emptied limbs peals an opera of moon.
This is the way we choose to love the world.

Steadiness

Margaret Gibson

Whether it's a wolf or a wasp we meet within it,
each moment asks first for our steadiness.

In the long dry summer just past, not the steadiest pond could hold
its level. Ours shrank down, baring its flag and clink stones

like fangs. Now in winter the water has seeped fully back and risen
to kiss the placid stones of the spillway—

the pond, now steady, a more generous world. Down under,
the bullfrogs have burrowed below the silt and rotted

lilies, content to sleep through the cold, deep or shallow.
No one asks their motives. No one asks if theirs

is a natural, or an acquired, humility. For the true contemplative,
as for a bodhisattva, gratitude holds steady, no matter what.

I'm doing my level best, echoes my mother,
years ago caught out, trembling in distress at some minor failing,

wanting to have what she didn't—a peaceful heart. I wish I had
held her hands until they stopped shaking. More calmly

now I reenter last night's dream, walking steadily through a barren
tract to offer my breast to the wolf—

revising the myth that gave us not self-mastery, but empire.

Indra and the Ants

Andrew Sydlik

Little black bodies march
atop the unclean countertop

stopping to drink at the sticky
stain of cherry Kool-Aid.

Each of these ants was once an Indra,
conquering god of the *Upanishads*,

who struck down serpent-demons
with lightning-bolt fury,

released waters to the Earth,
rewarded himself with opulent palace;

carpenter god lamenting,
"He is immortal – so are his desires!"

It took the combined will
of creator, destroyer, and preserver

to give Indra perspective.
When the boy in rags visited,

vaulted chambers rung with laughter,
marble floors crawled with insects—

"And you too will crawl,"
thundered his prophecy,

compelling the haughty god to yoga
to escape his insect destiny.

I think of all the war-glutted Indras
who can be student to my Vishnu,

so I bolt toward the door
to spread a lesson of humility.

Turning back to the procession, I note
the Indras seem quite happy

working together to taste
a bit of spilled cherry Kool-Aid.

I hold back judgment, open the fridge,
take out the pitcher to share with the world.

Ghazal   Deema K. Shehabi

for Marilyn Hacker

> *Your night is of lilac*
> —Mahmoud Darwish

Who crosses the road at night in shawls of lilac?
Again, we'll lash out at the future with all our lilac.

The girl wails over her father's body on a beach that hives
with warships as though she's dressed in fireballs of lilac.

Laila, bitten by ferocious longing, absorbs the oiled blood
of Qays' jasmine, measures the deep-carved sprawl of his lilac.

O lover of the tabla, your beat swelling with multitudes,
come rest your blue-veined hands on the scripted calls of lilac.

I will return one day, she says, to light the lamp of my snuffed-
out country, to translate the original protocol of lilac.

The Sufis say that everyone is to blame in a time of war
while they row their night boats towards waterfalls of lilac.

Shahid, how often did you "land on ashen tarmacs"
landing—then flying—your feet hauled by lilac?

Nothing is left for this parched earth where you are buried,
says the groom to his bride, except a rainfall of lilac.

If you don't let my son return to his mother, says the father
to the interrogator, your body will be mauled by lilac.

How we betrayed those summer clouds that crumpled our bed
      sheets;
our hasty unfolding, our constant footfalls towards lilac.

What have we lost, father, that can't be regained? What of our
      devotional
yearning beneath the overgrown walls of lilac?

Afternoon   **Emily K. Bright**

Two turtles, sunning mirrors of each other
with their yellow-pin-striped limbs displayed,
their striking pendant tails. The mother
turns her head to me, then looks past, unafraid.
A third, in water turned near see-through by
sun, casts each leg out smoothly turn by turn.
Not far to go and all day to arrive,
it swims, its pinched face lifted up to learn
how the surfaces taste throughout the long day.
I've seen them dive down slick as fish when spooked
and hold their air long minutes in the lake,
but now there's sun, the swimmer's patient strokes,
and bugs that land on heads soon fly away.
Shadows lengthen. Stillness is a choice you make.

Dandelions   Hayan Charara

The first time I picked a dandelion
I thought it must be symbolic.
It was the year
my father opened his *Beer & Wine*.
We moved out of our west side
neighborhood, away from the ugly trees
that hung over our heads
and kept us dark, from dogs
barking in the alleyway, from the sewers
where rats cried for escape.
And that year my mother
returned from a trip to Lebanon
where she saw her parents
for the first time in a decade.
But these didn't matter.
That yellow flower was symbolic
of something so simple,
so easy to overlook.
It was the hottest day in July.
Construction workers were putting
asphalt to the parking lot.
Hot tar from a rumbling truck
dumped onto the gravel,
and shirtless men smoothed it out.
The lot was now hard and black,
without a bump or crack,
except in one spot, near
the driveway heading into
Wyoming Avenue. Through layers
of rock, dirt, pebbles and stone,
a dandelion with bright petals
burst through, pushing aside
the pavement for fresh air
and sunlight. It grew strong
and full of color in a concrete jungle.
I picked it at the roots,
took it home and planted it
behind the garage beside the sunflowers.
My mother dug it out. "It's a weed,"

she said. But even that was all right.
Years later, I still see dandelions
where they're not supposed to be.
Driving down the Ford Freeway
after the snow has melted
and the clouds disappeared,
every now and then, alongside
the embankments, the dull grayness
of cars and bridges and viaducts
gets touched up with a little yellow.
It may look like litter, or even
an oasis in the city. But really,
it's a show of survival, of getting through,
of coming close to not making it,
and then, all of a sudden,
life where we never expect it.

Hard Bop   Barbara Crooker

It's a sweet June day, and the mockingbirds
are singing, as are the rubber tires of cars
on the road, and both of these sounds reverberate,
echo, the jazz of early summer, with the muffled
percussion of wind in the trees. A crow
twangs and plucks his big black bass,
and I'm riffing along with the breeze, scatting
words here and there, trying to make sense
of my life, and the news of the world—
almost daily, another car bomb shatters
the desert, and hundreds of lives are torn
apart, as grief ripples outward in concentric
rings. Thomas Merton said, *God is that bit
of diamond dust shining within each of us,*
scraps of stardrift, our shared DNA. What
new language now needs to be born, a fusion
of birdsong and sandstorm, an improv
of heartbeat's ratatatat and moonbeam's
glissando? Crows in the road. Tires in the rain.

All Things Falling   Holly J. Hughes

Consider how all things fall to this earth:
gravity's reach to galaxy-flung stars,
light skipping like a stone, time fractal,
shuddering strings of space, invisible.

Last swirl of maple leaf, twittering seeds,
puff of dandelion, deep drift of pyeweed,
osprey's barred feather, talon-gripped salmon
delicate mouse bones dropped by falcon.

Airplanes, missiles, cluster bombs:
the bodies they carry, the bodies
that send them, all falling through
the air which will not hold them,

which holds lightly
only star glint,
leaf swoon,
feather.

For the Blue Morpho   Holly J. Hughes

Tell me leaf cutter ants don't know the meaning
of *community,* don't communicate as they

carry the forest canopy on their backs,
green flags marking a trail of peace.

Tell me walking palms don't plan ahead,
sending long runners toward the sun,

that this green forest doesn't breathe,
bromeliads and epiphytes blossoming in thin air.

Tell me God doesn't have a sense of play;
that the toucan's bill is only for stealing eggs,

that she doesn't love primary colors best of all:
red, blue and yellow of the Scarlet Macaw.

Tell me she isn't here, flitting through the
long ropes of the fig on iridescent blue wings,

that the Resplendent Quetzal does not know
it is resplendent, from its yellow triangle beak

to its green sheen, blue waterfall of tail.
Tell me we aren't all infinitely variable, endlessly

evolving. And if we are, tell me
we can't find a way for all of us to live.

Blue Heron   Hedy Habra

An Egyptian sculpture
lost in the Northern wilderness,
the blue heron stands out
in the whitened landscape,
mimics an ibis' fixed stare,
studies the frozen creek,
sensing trembling gills
beneath the transparent sheet.

But why land in my backyard
I wonder, where no lotus ever grows?
Unless he sees his own ancestral roots
in my wide-open eyes lined with kohl,
and knows that water from the Nile
still runs in my veins since birth.

In warmer seasons he has seen me
feed the silver fish,
tend the vegetable garden,
bend over perennials
springing stronger each year,
add more seeds,
making this our home,

where we've lived the longest ever.

Today he saw me walk in circles
in the stillness of barren trees
over crisp snow flakes
masking all signs of life,
the forget-me-nots throbbing
under their icy coat, scintillating,

a thousand suns
opening a dam of flowing memories
on sunnier shores
promises of blossoms to come

until suddenly, as if pulsated by an engine,
statuesque, the migrant bird deploys gigantic
wings, disappears through the dead branches.

In the Open Country   Derek Sheffield

From the fingers of women
circled and humming
inches a rug, another crimson patch
for the world,

for the men in wool
raising hammers to stake the plain
where they will briefly live
among blue mountains.

Light levels like water
and they drop their work, kneel
before the rising earth,
thin shadows spiring,

gathering, another night
blackened with ashes of old fires
ignited by the scent of wet caves
you and I might remember.

This Day in Particular   Christina Lovin

A benediction: September 11, 2002

You mowed the mares' field yesterday
because the sky was clear, the air dry,
and would be so for days to come, or so
the *Farmer's Almanac* had claimed.

Today, the baler swept the field of loosely
mounded timothy and clover, swirling
up and over, tidying the strewn field,
leaving only stubble. "I haven't cut

the feet from off one rabbit," you say. I hear
the echoes of your mother's hills
in the modulation
of your voice, as you tell me of the time

a sucker snake was caught up, bound
into a bale, dying there, and how the hay,
pressed around the rotting flesh, would have decayed.
So you spread and fed it fresh to mares and foals

that leaned the fence beside the barn. You tell me
that too many horses spoil a tract of grass:
their droppings soil the hay,
rendering it inedible and sour.

You say there is a man you know who
sheared the legs from off twin fawns.
Hidden in the tall grass, startled to a run,
they skittered from the tractor's wheels, only

to meet the mower blade eight feet
to the side. How he didn't have a gun
but in plain sight of his grandsons, seven
and five, he hammered the deer skulls to death's

mercy. But today, not one rabbit, snake, or fawn.
No small child to witness. Only firm, fresh

bales that wait to be unbound and split
to ease winter-hungry bellies of animals

held stamping in their stalls or snowbound
in the fields. And in that cold
the fragrance of September's grass
will rise like prayer and you will not remember

this day in particular, just the rest that comes
at the end of the sweat, these blameless bales
towering to the haymow's
rafters, the sacred smell of the living

creatures, the blessed soil.

Explaining Current Events   Martha Silano
to a One-Year-Old

The sky will never be this gray—belly of a mallard,
body of a plane emerging from clouds—
layer upon layer in every direction.

Gone are the goldfinches, barn swallows, violet greens.
Welcome the juncos, their metronome calls,
welcome the play of light and dark,

the occasional patch of blue, the ever-present wind.
The dogwood's aflame. The big leaf maple's
right behind her. Lots of things

could easily ignite, which is why we dress you
in flame retardant pajamas, circle your neck
with light-blue hearts.

The larkspur we waited for all summer
is finally blooming, but it's wrong—
bent beneath a cedar, snaking up,

snaking right back down. When your eyes are closed,
I focus on your eyelids. Your eyelids
and your breath, breath of the wind,

the cottonwood's applause. Because you open like a flower,
I leave a light on in the hall. Because each day
the red in the leaves a little redder,

I wish they were more like lullabies of unknown origin—
like the one you wake from to cake and pretty horses.
To explain them, I need to explain

country, God, passion, loyalty, love.
Because I don't know how else
to begin, I begin with love.

Landscape in a Time of War   Chad Prevost

It's March and I go out into the streets before the sun rises to see
whatever life skuttles down the root-split sidewalks
and how the streetlights blink yellow
and the moon is a great white eye.
                              A mile later
I trek across Veteran's Bridge, and then it is only myself
crossing between cliffs,
                    a few stray clouds
beginning to fill with radiance
and lined-up U.S. flags flapping in the open cough
of the east.
                    The limestone walls of the half-drunk river
are a veteran's hardened arteries,
                         and factory smoke
      lifts like the promise
of a cancerous horizon, like the past floats across
tomorrow's canvas, a frayed flag
of resignation.
                    Cumulonimbus are bundling
behind Lookout Mountain like a gastric bypass,
like maybe the weather isn't just a symbol

for something larger than ourselves
                              but splits
          the open wound of the sky like this
to catch someone's attention.
                              Maybe the personified sky
is Nihilism's poster child, an impostor posing
as meaning, and so it doesn't mind
                              wasting itself
          upon the tin ears
of its unappreciative audience. Through the Iron Works'
opaque windows on the corner of Oak and MLK,
the yellow stacks of wasted news.
                              Veterans need more
          bridges like this, connecting cities
divided between themselves.
                              I turn around
before I get to the crazy bearded dude
clotting up an intersection's traffic,
                              waving his sign
in protest to the way we abort
the past like an unwanted child. The cross at his neck
dangles like a dog tag.
                              The personified river valley
might as well stand for itself—new engagements
with the fogged-over—the wind gusts
tangle a few flags, others in full-blown salute
to the infinite unknown dead
                              standing for something
larger than themselves.

Architecture

Chase Twichell

I peer into Japanese characters
as into faraway buildings
cut from the mind's trees.

In the late afternoon a small bird
shakes a branch, lets drop a white splash.

In the wind, in the rain,
the delicate wire cage glistens,
empty of suet.

Poetry's not window-cleaning.
It breaks the glass.

Becoming the Next Thread

Poems of Ritual & Vigil

Wrap in Parchment and Also Pink Paper   Angie Estes

Towards the end
of the third millennium B.C.,
the first images of the human face
were carved on limestone
slabs, late Neolithic funerary
figures, faces with no ears or

mouth—as if, in the place they were
headed, they'd have no desire
to speak or hear, never need to
eat. Everything that delighted,
whatever could excite—beads, flint
daggers, necklaces of shells—they buried

with their corpses, saying farewell
to pleasure because they believed
the next world would be just
like this one. And so the dead were
placed in the fetal position, waiting
to unfold again, tongues held

like viatica in the mouth. What can be
translated into heaven *should be high
& beautiful.* Because Mina Pächter
and the women of Terezín could not
be transported out of the ghetto
in which they starved, they talked

and even argued about the correct way
to prepare food they might never eat
again—*cooking with the mouth,*
they called it—and wrote their recipes
on whatever scraps of paper
they could find: *Like strudel, fill*

 *as desired. One can do everything
with* the body, *fill to your
liking,* but only what's legible
remains—like the bones

of the saints disinterred and
translated into reliquaries—while

the part that's in love with
God dissolves into *Cheap Rose Hip
Kisses*: *with the small spoon
make kisses on oblaten paper
and bake in a low oven.* What could be
carried across from Terezín was a recipe

for the end of a meal, translated
out of German: *War Dessert
7 boiled grated potatoes, 5-6 spoons
sugar, 2 spoons flour, 1 spoon cocoa,
2 spoons dry milk, 1 spoon [illegible],
1 knife point [illegible]. Bake slowly.*

Facing It   **Yusef Komunyakaa**

My black face fades,
hiding inside the black granite.
I said I wouldn't,
dammit: No tears.
I'm stone. I'm flesh.
My clouded reflection eyes me
like a bird of prey, the profile of night
slanted against morning. I turn
this way—the stone lets me go.
I turn that way—I'm inside
the Vietnam Veterans Memorial
again, depending on the light
to make a difference.
I go down the 58,022 names,
half-expecting to find
my own in letters like smoke.
I touch the name Andrew Johnson;
I see the booby trap's white flash.
Names shimmer on a woman's blouse

but when she walks away
the names stay on the wall.
Brushstrokes flash, a red bird's
wings cutting across my stare.
The sky. A plane in the sky.
A white vet's image floats
closer to me, then his pale eyes
look through mine. I'm a window.
He's lost his right arm
inside the stone. In the black mirror
a woman's trying to erase names:
No, she's brushing a boy's hair.

Weaving Peace   Judith Montgomery

Cross warp and weft close as kiss
to shape this cloth. Interlace floss

and filament to weave the one cloak
and shield that may harbor two bodies

bent under Himalayan winter. Shelter
three from scudding desert blaze and rage—

four from sharp stone seized and flung
in alley war. Offer each thread, prayer

on prayer to greet the warp—Asian silk,
more scarlet than wound or weeping—

Egyptian flax infused with silver grace—
Albertan lambs' wool, gleaming fresh

as spring-leaf. Only intersecting may this
finest web-work fill the loom with weight

and hue. Only as weaver after weaver
sets her hand, his hand, to the shuttle.

As each consents to cross and clasp thread
with given thread, close as mingled breath

across abyss. Come: approach the task:
this art. Lay heart and hand to wood

and wool. Become the loom. The shuttle.
Become the next thread.

Opening Cans   Robert Cording

After reading the news this morning,
I give thanks for a pile of dirty dishes
and the five loads of wash spawning
in the laundry room, and the mindless
hours of sorting and folding ahead.
Believe me, I relish the forced humility
of squaring fitted sheets; and to wed
unmatched white socks—a kind of sanity.
So let there be tasks for the daily chaos
of another suicide bombing, for the obscene
getting and spending that dispossess
each day. These few hours are serene.
Think of Hemingway's Nick: to withstand
the crazy hurts of war, he *liked to open cans.*

Household Gods

David Hassler

for Lynn

Funny how happiness doesn't need
words, but is more like humming,
a purr in the back of the throat.
When we're lucky, it declares us
home, climbing through a window,
following our steps from room to room,
like the cat that found you sitting
on the porch. It must have known where to go.
We were careful in naming him, knowing
he's been called by other names.

I feel lucky with you, as though
happiness could find us anywhere.
Driving today, we looked for
lawn ornaments and saw a giant Buddha.
We stepped around a pink flamingo, pudgy
cherubs, a figure of Jesus praying,
until we found, smiling back at us,
a statue of a woman carrying two baskets.
She was chipped with one arm half-broken.
We got her for a steal and placed her
in the garden, where we feel at home
on our knees, pulling weeds, pinching
aphids, praying against leaf wilt
and vine borer. Barefoot, she stands
between the mint and basil, repeating
the steady hum of green.

The Fourteen Happy Days   Dave Lucas

for Bob Beach

I have now reigned about fifty years in victory or peace,
beloved by my subjects, dreaded by my enemies, and
respected by my allies. Riches and honors, power and pleasure,
have waited on my call, nor does any earthly blessing appear
to have been wanting to my felicity. In this situation,
I have diligently numbered the days of pure and genuine happiness
which have fallen to my lot. They amount to fourteen.
        —Abd-ar-Rahman III, Caliph of Cordoba

A day of daylong sun, a day of rain,
a day when we ate berries on the branch.
The day my mother took me to the river
to rinse our clothes among the smooth-washed stones.
A day of hunting, ended without quarry.
The day we barely left the bed
but for the cold water that slaked us clear.
A day of solitary quiet. A night
we emptied bottles with our talk.
A day when I spoke only to myself.
A day my father toasted to my health.
A day we made a meal of what was left
from other days. Two nights of nightlong sleep.
The day the dog rested his head in my lap.

How to Draw a Horse   Robert Miltner

after a linocut by Marc Snyder

Begin with a pyramid. With an Egyptian riding a horse across the
sandy expanse, planning to have his cats and liver accompany him
to the afterlife, a place where honey never goes bad.

After the Israelites leave, the British will arrive, pockets stuffed
with guns and laws, filling the coal cars with pirated mummies
they'll toss into the locomotive's fire, fuel for the Colonial train.

But today the Egyptian basks in the sun like a sphinx, head held
high, centered in a momentary universe. A cloud briefly covers
the sun like an eye patch, then passes. Leaving only a horse.

At the Veterans Hospital   Katharyn Howd Machan

In Aphrodite's deep and fullest hue
I dance again the halls of Ares' breath
and touch the shadows, celebrating *who*
instead of *what* within these walls of death.
My ankles offer golden bells that sing
of light and wonder, as my hands reach out
rich rhythm-echo of bright zills that ring
the names of Love, close whisper to far shout.
How is it War can use a man like stone
to crush another, smiling proud and bold,
then drop him cracked and breaking, left alone
to crumble into dust as he grows old?
Again I whirl, my hot pink veil held high
to every trembling smile, each waking eye.

Turn

Lisa Rosen

Comfort hides
in the edges of things

powdered panels of Juicy Fruit
that cheered our mouths before school
slipped from Nellie's pocket.

The fringe of my father's tallis
gentling a room of dark-suited devotions

the way stroking a blanket's brim
smoothes the way to sleep.

I turn in the long sleeve
of this world, without any need
to wrestle its seam.

All the Way Up

Lisa Rosen

flowers float like pale stars
in the grass, and at the top
of the hill there's a plank
of wood hanging from an oak.

I lift myself into its level lap,
a pendulous Sabbath where
branches curve and meet,
framing landscapes.

Blow sweet shadows,
there's no holding back
the light, it curls
through the leaves
and snapping grasses. It pads

along Queen Anne's lace.
Someone with faith in roots

and a weathered limb,
cut, carried, measured and

slipped sleeves of rubber
over rope, knotted it so I'm swinging
between hayfield and cloud.
Someone I will never know
is blessing me.

Carving   Jeanne Bryner

I am not the first woman
to kneel beside opal river mist.
In my arms' basket, baby daughter is sky
her lips are petals, they circle the flute
of my nipple, undone, my braids swish,
tails of sorrel horses grazing in a field.
Back, back, my head tilts
while my mother, my daughter's
grandmother washes my hair.
Sun becomes a yellow blanket,
it covers us, the baby's a loaf of warm bread.
She sleeps, without thinking, our bodies glide
like waves over sand, softly, mother sings to the clouds,
our hands do the ancient dance of morning.
High above us, my sister perches on her rock,
blade to wood, she carves the moment,
quiet hummingbird, wren, golden eagle,
the milk rising, the water coming down.

Surrender

Alice Cone

Soft cotton, white—

Should I unfold the bolt
and cut a swath? What shape?

To stitch a hem around the fray
before I wave or run
the fabric up the pole
would feign control—
and this is loosening.
Allow the edges to unravel—
and shake the cloth out, whole.

Canvas of winter—sky,
sea, prairie.
An expanse—
endless as potential.

        (What flags is not belief—
        but certain notions
        concerned with outcome.)

And so I would unfurl a spotless carpet
down the aisle, float to the altar
swaddled in such lace as this
material might unveil—bridal.

I cast my prayer
into the wind;
the answer threads itself
into my skin.

Firewood   Richard Hague

for Joe

Sometimes I leave some
stacked at the foot
of a hickory or poplar
far down in the woods.
That way, walking,
idly discovering a pile next year
or ten years from now,
I'll remember an August afternoon,
and how peace followed
the racket of my saw.

Or even better:
a stranger,
come up from the creek alone,
ten miles trudged some icy winter day,
hunkering down here
with some tinder
and a match.

His hands.
The slow joy in his eyes.
The community of the world.

Blue Flame   Stephen Haven

February 2003

When the sun is rising and my seven-year-old
catches it through the trees, and we sit
at the table, his slow oatmeal, my slow jam
and coffee, a dull magenta arching
in the horizon's nook, and a sharp
steel-eyed blue above it,
and blue the hottest part of the flame,
I know we live under the light touch

of heaven's scam. Or is it our own
tempering, heaven's stain?
Something chars us down from there:
The day comes soft shoeing,
all doe-eyed, the womb's wonder
of the sky. But in its slow time,
what will the battered
yoke of the dawn
sizzle in each emptying house?

In a minute, from the microwave,
the green digital flash of a school day.

All is quiet here, but somewhere
the flick of a candle sears
through rafters. Somewhere,
half a day and half the world away,
the red flag of morning snaps
at half-mast above our own
holy fire as it conjugates itself
across a cross-less altar.
Not here. Not now. It is, after all,

Ohio, and given the state of things,
the thermometer quivers into single
digits and everything slips
to its opposite. Cold burns.

The morning's hot celestial wax
drips into the seal of our
rushed footprints. In the boy-warmth

of the kitchen, absent for a moment,
the wet of our breath against glass,
this stirred bowl, this daily crust.

If a Bodhisattva   David Budbill

If a Bodhisattva is one who, although enlightened,
chooses to remain here in this suffering world and

be with The Suffering People, then there is no escape
for any of us, since how could we gain enlightenment

by running away from the pain and injustice that is
all around us? To decide simply to remove yourself

from the fray, to sit down and find peace at the center
of a storm by ignoring the causes of that storm can't

possibly be a way to any understanding, for if such is
impossible for a Bodhisattva how much more impossible

for the temporal and worldly likes of you and me?

Touch Each Letter

Marilynn Rashid

After reading the article about Darfur,
I look for the atlas, wanting to know,
to touch, to see—to do one small thing
about my ignorance, since I feel powerless
to do anything about anyone else's.
I barely get the book off the shelf
when I am called to help my second-grader,
with his spelling words, those that begin with *wh*—
why and where and when and who, and what,
I say to myself, is the point of pushing this
on my seven-year-old, this *-h-* that hardly speaks,
if at all, and yet, I think, what luxury
to have this time in life to teach him
the simple technique his teachers describe—
say the word, touch each letter (as I want to touch
the map), write it down, repeat it. What children
and whose eyes will never struggle with a word?
Whose hands will not touch letter or leaf?
How to see, to touch each one, to know who they were
or would become—who and where and when and why.
The silence of the *-h-* can haunt you, its meager aspiration
could blow you down, and so those other words
come bombing in around me: death squad, rape,
ethnic cleansing, genocide. Name it, say the word,
touch each letter, repeat it, write it down.

Gentleness that Wears Away Rock

Poems of Meditation & Prayer

For the Children   Gary Snyder

The rising hills, the slopes,
of statistics
lie before us.
the steep climb
of everything, going up,
up, as we all
go down.

In the next century
or the one beyond that,
they say,
are valleys, pastures,
we can meet there in peace
if we make it.

To climb these coming crests
one word to you, to
you and your children:

stay together
learn the flowers
go light

Pray for Peace   Ellen Bass

Pray to whomever you kneel down to:
Jesus nailed to his wooden or plastic cross,
his suffering face bent to kiss you,
Buddha still under the bo tree in scorching heat,
Adonai, Allah. Raise your arms to Mary
that she may lay her palm on our brows,
to Shekinah, Queen of Heaven and Earth,
to Inanna in her stripped descent.

Then pray to the bus driver who takes you to work.
On the bus, pray for everyone riding that bus,
for everyone riding buses all over the world.

Drop some silver and pray.

Waiting in line for the movies, for the ATM,
for your latte and croissant, offer your plea.
Make your eating and drinking a supplication.
Make your slicing of carrots a holy act,
each translucent layer of the onion, a deeper prayer.

To Hawk or Wolf, or the Great Whale, pray.
Bow down to terriers and shepherds and Siamese cats.
Fields of artichokes and elegant strawberries.

Make the brushing of your hair
a prayer, every strand its own voice,
singing in the choir on your head.
As you wash your face, the water slipping
through your fingers, a prayer: Water,
softest thing on earth, gentleness
that wears away rock.

Making love, of course, is already prayer.
Skin, and open mouths worshipping that skin,
the fragile cases we are poured into.

If you're hungry, pray. If you're tired.
Pray to Gandhi and Dorothy Day.
Shakespeare. Sappho. Sojourner Truth.

When you walk to your car, to the mailbox,
to the video store, let each step
be a prayer that we all keep our legs,
that we do not blow off anyone else's legs.
Or crush their skulls.
And if you are riding on a bicycle
or a skateboard, in a wheelchair, each revolution
of the wheels a prayer as the earth revolves:
less harm, less harm, less harm.
And as you work, typing with a new manicure,
a tiny palm tree painted on one pearlescent nail,
or delivering soda or drawing good blood

into rubber-capped vials, twirling pizzas—

With each breath in, take in the faith of those
who have believed when belief seemed foolish,
who persevered. With each breath out, cherish.

Pull weeds for peace, turn over in your sleep for peace,
feed the birds, each shiny seed
that spills onto the earth, another second of peace.
Wash your dishes, call your mother, drink wine.

Shovel leaves or snow or trash from your sidewalk.
Make a path. Fold a photo of a dead child
around your Visa card. Scoop your holy water
from the gutter. Gnaw your crust.
Mumble along like a crazy person, stumbling
your prayer through the streets.

Proposal   **Fady Joudah**

I think of god as a little bird who takes
To staying close to the earth,
The destiny of little wings
To exaggerate the wind
And peck the ground.

I see Haifa
By my father and your father's sea,
The sea with little living in it,
Fished out like a land.

I think of a little song and
How there must be a tree.

I choose the sycamore
I saw split in two
Minaret trunks on the way
To a stone village, in a stone-thrower mountain.

Were the villagers wrong to love
Their donkeys and wheat for so long,
To sing to the good stranger
Their departure song?

I think of the tree that is a circle
In a straight line, future and past.
I wait for the wind to send
God down, I become ready for song.

I sing, in a tongue not my own:
We left our shoes behind and fled.
We left our scent in them
Then bled out our soles.
We left our mice and lizards

There in our kitchens and on the walls.
But they crossed the desert after us,
Some found our feet in the sand and slept,
Some homed in on us like pigeons,
Then built their towers in a city coffin for us...

I will probably visit you there after Haifa.
A little bird to exaggerate the wind

And lick the salt off the sea of my wings. I think

God reels the earth in when the sky rains
Like fish on a wire.

And the sea, each time it reaches the shore,
Becomes a bird to see of the land
What it otherwise wouldn't.
And the wind through the trees
Is the sea coming home.

Turtle Blessing

Penny Harter

After the boy threw the pregnant turtle
hard against the brick wall
of the courtyard, screaming
"What are you, some kind of
fucking humanitarian?"
to the girl who called him crazy,
the creature bounced off,
crawled a few feet, blood
seeping into the weeds
from her cracked shell,
and stopped.

She died last night,
was buried, her eggs gone
with her into the earth.

This morning in the mist
by Seeley's Pond, an ancient turtle,
huge and black on the wet grass,
turns its blunt head this way, that,
as it crawls up the slope
toward the road, and I bless it
against the crunch of its dark shell,
against the driver who will not swerve.

Zazen

Jennifer Karmin

name the parts
of the body
used for prayer

notice buddha's hands
when they are touching
open
closed

notice your hands
the way you touch
yourself
others
cover your eyes

notice
birds
wind
the smell of air

take pictures
in your mind

record time

Rock Bottom

Kim Jensen

I still believe
in the power of words.

The shiver
of aspen leaves

on the bank of the river
send their own message—

the use of any sword
is a violation of every law.

Isn't it punishment enough
to endure

this wreckage of a human
story? tossed back and forth

on too many bodies
of teachings

awash
until the fall.

On that last tumble downwards
there's no room

for interpretation. Praise the brave
who take the plunge

and trade every article of faith
for a shred of compassion or reason—

either one.

Songs for a Belgrade Baker   Karen Kovacik

> With electricity cut by NATO bombs, she waits in candlelight
> for her customers.—*New York Times* photo caption, May 24, 1999

Reportage
Her shoulders ache. In ten minutes they will wander in
from the cellars, wanting breakfast for the children,
a sandwich loaf, something crusty that would stand up
to soup. The line will curl through the dark shop.
They will point, choose, and their purchases she will tally
by hand. Later, there'll be a rock concert, a rally.
By then, if she's lucky, she'll be asleep under feathers,
dreaming of the tiny horns named for cuckolds and whether
they will lose their curl in the ovens, for the young ones,
deprived of Ninja Turtles, are hungry for these pointy buns.

Corporeal
This is my body, this is yours
The sour mother rising in the bowl
will bring forth fingers, horns, and plaits
O armpit of pumpernickel, groin of corn
give it to us black and blonde
Sink into the beds of our bellies
and grow us new bones

Folkloric
Offer it with salt to welcome a weary traveller
Sign each braid with a cross before baking
He who steps on a crumb will make the souls in limbo weep
Drop a slice on the floor—kiss it before eating
Salute the bride with a loaf, and she will be happy in bed

Antiphonal
Blessed are the Slovenes, for they are the cake-makers
Blessed are the Croats, for they excel at fish
Blessed the Macedonians, for their black wine gave birth to
        philosophy
Blessed, too, the Bosnians for the subtlety of their tongues—who
        else would season veal with lemon and hibiscus?
Blessed the Herzegovinians, for their silver wine strengthens
        friendships
Blessed the Serbs, for their bean soup makes foreign clerics sweat
Blessed the Albanians for their love of cinnamon
And blessed are the olive trees and vineyards, goats and sheep,
        for they serve both parable and table
Blessed are the mint and dill, for they are the peacemakers
And blessed the yeast and sponge, the sour-gray loaves, for they
        have inherited the earth

Kwansaba for June Jordan   Mary E. Weems

June Jordan would be dumping word bombs
on the White House like D-Day in
America, wailing verbs like an elder blues
singer, hitting that one right note each
night—If she wasn't busy filling God
in on all the ways the world
needs to collect like clouds, rain change.

Wind   Ahimsa Timoteo Bodhrán

Sing from the back
of your throat, out each nostril. Flare
in retention, bone beyond cartilage.

Smoke fills our lungs;
ceremony. Deep tones,
towards the fire and back, tobacco released
from palm
toward each direction, we circle

round. Serpents
tongue the sky, lick for moisture, north,
rain; mosquitos. We are
not the only dancers.

Coral webbings, single hooves, paddles,
flips, stubs, only distant
memories of legs, dwell in my ear, vibrate,
dip down to root tap.
River through my canyon. Bead my brow.

Plants rattle to
the ground, seed pods wither and
burst; dry, sinking in, sought soil,
tunneling to fire. Perfume
of the body, we kiss by smelling.
Renewed, leaving

dried on skin, marking
shared territories, marred skin,
pores flooded, without wounding
(those are other rituals, fire-tipped,
of piercing and pulse).

I take you in by breathing

through
each motion,
deeper into emptiness, full
feathers flap, down my back

this place the clouds have hidden.

Seeded.

Snow
falls

into the fire.

We mist up,
and grace the sky.

May the Feather of Justice,
The Waters of Eternity,
& The Wingèd Circle of Peace

grant you vast measures
of creativity
& consolation

Prayer from a Picket Line   Daniel Berrigan

Bring the big guardian
angels or devils in black
jackets and white casques
into the act at last. *Love, love at the end.*

The landholders withholding
no more; the jails springing
black and white Eastern men;
truncheons like lilies, hoses
gentle as baby pee. *Love, love at the end.*

Bishops down in the ranks
mayors making it too.
Sheriff meek as a shorn lamb
smelling like daisies, drinking dew.
Love, love at the end.

Prayer for the Morning Headlines   Daniel Berrigan

MERCIFULLY GRANT PEACE IN OUR DAYS THROUGH
YOUR HELP MAY WE BE FREED FROM PRESENT
DISTRESS. HAVE MERCY ON WOMEN AND CHILDREN,
HOMELESS IN FOUL WEATHER, RANTING LIKE BEES
AMONG GUTTED BARNS AND STILES. HAVE MERCY ON
THOSE (LIKE US) CLINGING ONE TO ANOTHER UNDER
FIRE. HAVE MERCY ON THE DEAD, BEFOULED,
TRODDEN LIKE SNOW IN HEDGES AND THICKETS. HAVE
MERCY, DEAD MAN, WHOSE GRANDIOSE GENTLE HOPE
DIED ON THE WING, WHOSE BODY STOOD LIKE A TREE
BETWEEN STRIKE AND FALL, STOOD LIKE A CRIPPLE ON
HIS WOODEN CRUTCH. WE CRY: **HALT!** WE CRY:
PASSWORD! DISHONORED HEART, REMEMBER AND
REMIND, THE OPEN SESAME: FROM THERE TO HERE,
FROM INNOCENCE TO US: **HIROSHIMA DRESDEN
GUERNICA SELMA SHARPEVILLE COVENTRY
DACHAU VIETNAM AFGHANISTAN IRAQ.** INTO OUR
HISTORY, PASS! SEED HOPE. FLOWER PEACE.

The Book of Constellations   Michael Waters

Dominican Republic

We'd forgotten, again, *The Book of Constellations*,
so stretched on sand, unable
to finger even one winter warrior, to sketch one
creature lumbering shaggily
past muted heroes assembled star by star by God.
Or by man who squints below,
imposing myth in fearful murk upon far heavens.
No brilliance here. One hand stalks
crabwise into yours as husked coconuts plunge earthward.
We attempt slight revisions:
naming constellations after less mythical beings
who ruined our half-century
by harming helpless creatures left briefly in their charge:
Idi Amin, Ceausescu,
Marcos, Pinochet, the Papa Docs and Baby Docs,
that hypocritical fool
Strom Thurmond dragged to hell fifty-three years past his time,
Pope John Paul—but then we stop.
When did human love mutate into this reptilian
seething that makes us despise
ourselves? *Whose hand in mine?* So we revise: Noguchi,
Miles, Allen Ginsberg, Balthus,
Joe Strummer, Raymond Carver, Muriel Rukeyser,
Bob Marley and Audre Lorde!—
heroic trespassers thrumming heaven's negative
spaces, prodding the icy
stars to wheel once more and assume fierce grandeur with each
invocation of their names,
who kindle such generative, indelible fires
across the universe, *yes*,
our only universe, dear God, beloved, amen.

The Poets

Elmaz Abinader has won the 2002 Goldies Award for Literature, and PEN/ Josephine Miles award for poetry. Author of a memoir, *Children of the Roojme* (University of Wisconsin Press), she also authored *The Water Cycle*, and a novel, *When Silence was Frightening,* forthcoming. She is a co-founder of the Voices of Our Nations Arts Foundation and teaches at Mills College. "Peace is in the house, in the prayer and storytelling, in the cooking and conversation, in the quiet eyes of children, the hands of the mother, the crack of the window and squeak of the floorboard. Peace, like poetry, is the details."

Taha Muhammad Ali (born 1931) is a leading Palestinian poet. He and his family fled to Lebanon during the 1948-1949 Arab-Israeli war, during which their village was destroyed. Since the 1950s, Ali has lived in Nazareth and operated a souvenir shop outside the Church of Annunciation. His recent collection, *So What: New & Selected Poems, 1971–2005*, has brought him international acclaim.

Yehuda Amichai (1924-2000) was born in Germany and emigrated to Palestine in 1935. After having fought in World War II and Israel's War of Independence, Amichai became an active proponent of peace and reconciliation with the Arabs. He published dozens of volumes of poetry, and is widely considered the greatest modern Israeli poet. It has been said that if the Israeli/Palestinian conflict were to end, Amichai and Mahmoud Darwish would have received Nobel Peace Prizes.

Ellen Bass (Santa Cruz, CA) is the author of *The Human Line* (Copper Canyon Press, 2007). She co-edited (with Florence Howe) the groundbreaking *No More Masks! An Anthology of Poems by Women.* She quotes Mahatma Gandhi: "Whatever you do will be insignificant, but it is very important that you do it."

Joan E. Bauer (Pittsburgh, PA & Laguna Beach, CA) is associate editor of *Only the Sea Keeps: Poetry of the Tsunami* (Bayeux Arts, 2005), and her book of poetry, *The Almost Sound of Drowning,* will be published by Main Street Rag in November 2008. She quotes Martin Luther King, Jr.: "True peace is not merely the absence of tension; it is the presence of justice."

Daniel Berrigan (born 1921) is a poet, peace activist and Jesuit priest. During the 1960s, Berrigan participated in the Catonsville Nine action, which involved the raiding of a draft office and the burning of draft files with homemade napalm to protest against the Vietnam War. In his statement about the reason for their act, he wrote: "Our apologies, dear friends, for the fracture of good order, the burning of paper instead of children, the angering of the orderlies in the front parlor of the charnel house. We could not, so help us God, do otherwise." A key figure in the Plowshares Movement, committing acts of civil disobedience at nuclear sites to protest the nuclear weapons, he continues to be an outspoken leader of the peace movement.

Wendell Berry (born 1934) has lived most of his adult life farming and writing in Port Royal, Kentucky. In addition to being a fiction writer and poet, he is an astute critic of American culture, as seen in recent books *The Way of Ignorance* (2005) and *Blessed Are the Peacemakers: Christ's Teachings of Love, Compassion, and Forgiveness* (Shoemaker & Hoard, 2005). A recommended poetry collection by Berry is *A Timbered Choir: The Sabbath Poems,* (1998). "The care of the Earth is our most ancient and most worthy, and after all our most pleasing responsibility.To cherish what remains of it and to foster its renewal is our only hope."

Robert Bly (born 1926) has written over forty volumes of poetry, translations, and prose, and has been a key figure in the anti-war movement. In 1966 he co-founded American Writers Against the Vietnam War, which conducted readings throughout the country. During the ceremony for the National Book Award, which he won for *The Light Around the Body* (Harper & Row,1967), he handed over the $10,000 check to the Resistance. In 2008, he was named the Poet Laureate of Minnesota.

Ahimsa Timoteo Bodhrán (East Lansing, MI) is the author of *Yerbabuena/ Mala yerba, All My Roots Need Rain: mixed blood poetry & prose* (forthcoming). "Sharing our words, artistry, and reality as queer people of color, Indigenous peoples, and women of color helps create the world we envision for our peoples.

John Bradley (DeKalb, IL) teaches at Northern Illinois University and is the author of *Terrestrial Music* (Curbstone Press, 2006). "In times of terrorism and 'endless war,' we desperately need poetry in our daily lives."

Mark Brazaitis (Morgantown, WV) is the author of *The River of Lost Voices: Stories from Guatemala*, winner of the 1998 Iowa Short Fiction Award. A former Peace Corps Volunteer, he lives in Morgantown, West Virginia, with his wife and two daughters. "I believe that peace in this century will depend, to a great extent, on how well we care for the environment."

Emily K. Bright (Minneapolis, MN) is the author of *Glances Back* (Pudding House Press). "I believe that creative writing is a natural way of spreading peace and the work of human rights."

Jeanne Bryner (Newton Falls, OH) is the author of *No Matter How Many Windows,* forthcoming from Wind Publications in Kentucky. "I believe the reading and writing of poetry is sacred."

David Budbill (Wolcott, VT) has a book of poems *While We've Still Got Feet* from Copper Canyon Press (2005) and a pamphlet, *Nine Taoist Poems* (Longhouse Publishers, 2007). His most recent play is *A Song for My Father*. "To be politically engaged, as part of movements for peace and justice, is, or ought to be, a natural part of any poet's life."

C. P. Cavafy (1863-1933), a Greek man born in Alexandria, Egypt, worked as a civil servant while writing poetry, though in relative obscurity. Now known as one of the greatest Greek poets, Cavafy deals with both grand historical themes and intimate desire with equal delicacy and nuance.

Dane Cervine (Santa Cruz CA) has received awards from Adrienne Rich and Tony Hoagland. His recent book of poetry is *The Jeweled Net of Indra*

(Plain View Press, 2008). "Of peace and poetry, that the latter must strive to shape and seduce human consciousness to seek the former."

Hayan Charara (Houston,TX) is the author of two books, *The Alchemist's Diary* (Hanging Loose, 2001) and *The Sadness of Others* (Carnegie Mellon, 2006). He is editor of *Inclined to Speak: An Anthology of Contemporary Arab American Poetry* (University of Arkansas, 2008). Born in Detroit, he is also a woodworker. "I defer to Alan Watts, who said it much better than I ever have: 'Peace can be made only by those who are peaceful, and love can be shown only by those who love. No work of love will flourish out of guilt, fear, or hollowness of heart, just as no valid plans for the future can be made by those who have no capacity for living now.'"

Robert Cording (Worcester, MA) teaches English and creative writing at College of the Holy Cross where he is the Barrett Professor of Creative Writing. He has published five collections of poems, including *What Binds Us To This World* (Copper Beech Press, 1991), *Heavy Grace*, (Alice James, 1996), *Against Consolation* (CavanKerry Press, 2002), and most recently, *Common Life* (CavanKerry Press, 2006). "'Every day,' said Rabbi Nachman of Bratslav, 'the glory is ready to emerge from debasement.'"

Alice Cone (Kent, OH) teaches creative writing at Kent State University. Her poetry has appeared most recently in the *Penguin Review*, and her second chapbook of poems is *As If a Leaf Could Be Preserved* (Finishing Line Press 2006). "I believe that writing poetry can help a person come to some sort of peace with herself or himself—where all peace must begin—and that reading poetry can help a person move beyond rigid ways of thinking into a broader understanding."

Robert Creeley (1926-2005), born in Arlington, Massachusetts, was author of more than sixty books. Associated with the Black Mountain poets and his friend Charles Olson, Creeley won the Bollingen Prize for poetry, a Lannan Award for Lifetime Achievement, and was the Poet Laureate of New York from 1989-1991. Because of his strong opposition to the Vietnam War, Creeley refused to write about the war, arguing that war had already damaged so much else. Yet in "John's Song," he writes: "No more war, dear brother,/ no more, no more war/ if ever there is."

Barbara Crooker (Fogelsville, PA) is the author of *Line Dance* (Word Press, 2008). She has been a peace activist since 1963: involved in the Civil Rights and Anti-Vietnam War movements in the sixties, environmental activism in the 70s and 80s. "In the last election, I worked for Move-On and America Coming Together. I'm still hoping for a just and better world."

Jim Daniels (Pittsburgh, PA) is the author of these recent books of poems: *Street* (Bottom Dog Press, 2007) and *In Line for the Exterminator* (Wayne State University Press, 2008). "In these poems, I try to focus on how the Iraq War affects our daily lives here in Pittsburgh."

Diane di Prima (San Francisco, CA) is the author of 43 books of poetry and prose. A prime mover during The Beat Movement, her work has been translated into more than 20 languages. An expanded edition of her

Revolutionary Letters with 23 new poems has been released by Last Gasp Press, 2007.

Mahmoud Darwish (1941-2008) was born in the town of al-Birwe in Palestine and fled to Lebanon during the "nakba," or catastrophe. When his family returned to the new state of Israel, their village had been completely destroyed. Darwish was first a member of the Israeli communist party and then the Palestine Liberation Organization. He lived in exile for most of his life, publishing nearly forty volumes of poetry and prose. He is widely regarded as the greatest Palestinian poet.

Todd Davis (Bellwood, PA) has recently published *Some Heaven* (Michigan State University Press, 2008). "It's hard to take the life of another person while reading or writing a poem. Poetry demands contemplation, a quieting of so much that rages in us. It all comes down to: 'But I tell you who hear me: Love your enemies, do good to those who hate you, bless those who curse you, pray for those who mistreat you. If someone strikes you on one cheek, turn to him the other also. If someone takes your cloak, do not stop him from taking your tunic. Give to everyone who asks you, and if anyone takes what belongs to you, do not demand it back. Do to others as you would have them do to you' (Luke 6: 27-31)."

Emily Dickinson, (1830-1886, Amherst, MA) was a prolific though private poet who published little during her lifetime but is now seen as a major voice of modern and contemporary poetry. "A word is dead when it is said, some say. I say it just begins to live that day."

Edward A. Dougherty (Corning, NY) was a volunteer for two and a half years at a peace center in Hiroshima and is now teaching at Corning Community College. He is the author of four chapbooks of poetry, the latest being *The Luminous House* (Finishing Line Press, 2007), and two collections, *Pilgrimage to a Gingko Tree* (WordTech, 2008) and *Part Darkness, Part Breath* (Plain View Press, 2008).

Angele Ellis (Pittsburgh, PA) is the author of *Arab on Radar* (Six Gallery Press, 2007) and a 2008 recipient of a fellowship from the Pennsylvania Council on the Arts. Her poems have been featured in *Mizna, Grasslimb, Rune, Pittsburgh City Paper*, and *Voices from the Attic, Volume XIV*. "I believe that peace—as Rilke said of the future—'must enter into us, in order to transform itself in us, long before it happens.'"

Martín Espada (born 1957) learned political activism from his Puerto Rican father, and worked as a tenant lawyer and a supervisor of a legal services program. He has edited two important anthologies, including *Poetry Like Bread: Poets of the Political Imagination from Curbstone Press* (Curbstone Press, 1994) and eight books of his own poetry, most recently *The Republic of Poetry* (W.W. Norton, 2006).

Angie Estes (Worthington, OH) is the author of *Chez Nous* (Oberlin College Press, 2005). For her, Gertrude Stein says it best: "Loving repeating is one way of being."

Lawrence Ferlinghetti (San Francisco, CA) is the co-founder of City Lights Book Shop & Publishers. An author of poetry, translations, experimental fiction, theatre and criticism. His *A Coney Island of the Mind* (New Directions 1958) has sold over 1 million copies. A veteran of WW II, he has stood in opposition to American policies of war for 5 decades. His most recent book is *Poetry as Insurgent Art* (New Directions, 2007). "Poetry the common carrier/ for the transportation of the public/ to higher places/ than other wheels can / carry it./ Poetry still falls from the skies / into our streets still open."

Carolyn Forché (born 1950) is the author of four books of poetry, including *The Country Between Us* (Harper Perennial, 1982) which reflects on her time working as a journalist in El Salvador in the mid 1980s. She was the editor of a crucial anthology, *Against Forgetting: Twentieth Century Poetry of Witness* (1993), which collects the work of poets from around the globe who confronted the historical traumas of our time.

Allen Frost (Bellingham, WA) is a librarian at Western Washington University and is working on a new book of prose poems; his most recent title is *Another Life* (Bird Dog Publishing, 2007).

Margaret Gibson (Preston, CT) has authored the memoir, *The Prodigal Daughter* (University of Missouri Press) and nine books of poetry from LSU Press, most recently *One Body* (2007). "We need to live our lives as we write our poems: by calling on the power of imagination; by engaging in a constructive struggle with words, yoking sound and sense, thought and feeling, witness and vision; and by caring enough for the truth we want others to hear that we say it with honesty, with compassion, and with as much clarity as we can."

Gail Hosking Gilberg (Rochester, NY) is the author of the memoir *Snake's Daughter: The Roads in and out of War* (University of Iowa Press, 1997). Her poetry and essays have appeared in newspapers and literary journals for nearly two decades. "For me, poetry begins to touch the silence within, the one that has no other language, the one seeking peace."

Allen Ginsberg (1926-1997) burst onto the literary scene when *Howl and Other Poems* (City Lights, 1955), his first book, went on trial for obscenity charges. Ginsberg became a spokesperson for the counterculture and was a leader in the peace movement throughout his life. During the confrontations between police and Vietnam War protestors and at the 1968 Democratic National Convention in Chicago, Ginsberg chanted "om" for hours to calm the crowd. His book, *Wichita Vortex Sutra*, is a classic anti-war text that confronts the way in which war is waged on the level of language.

Hedy Habra (Kalamazoo, MI) received her MFA and a PhD in Spanish from Western Michigan University. Her poetry and fiction in French, Spanish and English appear in many journals and anthologies. "Poetry is an ever expanding stained glass formed by a diversity of colors, shapes and textures, creating a harmonious whole that encompasses time and space, in which we can see ourselves reflected as we delve into each of its disparate parts."

Richard Hague (Cincinnati, OH) is a poet, essayist, and fiction writer. His *Public Hearings*, containing political and satirical poems, is forthcoming from Word Press in 2009. He teaches in Cincinnati and Boston. "Poetry needs to acknowledge the existence of the political world as much as it does the world of nature or culture. People dismissive of political poetry are people who have forgotten Whitman's 'omnes, omnes, omnes.'"

Sam Hamill (Port Townsend, WA) is a founder of Copper Canyon Press, and following his protest to read at the White House edited *Poets Against the War* with Sally Anderson (Thunder's Mouth Press/ Nation Books 2003). "A government is a government of words, and when those words are used to mislead, to instill fear or to invite silence, it is the duty of every poet to speak fearlessly and clearly."

Penny Harter (Summit, NJ) is the author of *The Night Marsh* (WordTech Editions in 2008). "It is time to write poems that go beyond the personal, that speak for the Earth and its inhabitants in a time of great vulnerability for all species, and for the planet, itself, since all beings exist as integral and interconnected parts of the larger community of the universe."

David Hassler (Kent, OH) is the author of two books of poems, most recently, *Red Kimono, Yellow Barn* (Cloudbank Books, 2005). With photographer Gary Harwood he is the author of *Growing Season: The Life of a Migrant Community* (Kent State University Press, 2007). He is the Program and Outreach Director for the Wick Poetry Center at Kent State University. "I encourage students to discover how poems have been used to preserve the stories and insights of people from different cultures, so they can learn to share and preserve the stories of their own lives."

Stephen Haven (Ashland, OH) authored the memoir *The River Lock: One Boy's Life along the Mohawk* (Syracuse University Press) and the poems of *The Long Silence of the Mohawk Carpet Smokestacks* (West End Press/ University of New Mexico Press, 2004). "The experience of becoming a father returned me to my religious roots again. I believe with my whole being that 'the peace that passes understanding' is one of the profound ideas in human history and as difficult to achieve as it is central to a life lived fully."

William Heyen (Brockport, NY) His *Shoah Train: Poems* (Etruscan Press, 2003) was a finalist for the National Book Award in 2004. His most recent book is *A Poetics of Hiroshima & Other Poems* (Etruscan Press 2008). "Peace with our planet and among our species will take us, right now, about seven billion poems. I'd like to be one of them."

Jane Hirshfield, born in New York; after receiving her BA from Princeton University in their first graduating class to include women, she went on to study at the San Francisco Zen Center. Her books of poetry include *After* (HarperCollins, 2006) and *Given Sugar, Given Salt* (HarperCollins, 2001). Her book of essays is *Nine Gates: Entering the Mind of Poetry*. "One of the jobs of poets is to keep making those holding words available, so that when other people need them they will be there."

Holly J. Hughes (Indianola & Chimacum WA) and her chapbook *Boxing the Compass* (Floating Bridge Press) recently won the Floating Bridge chapbook award. "A poet I greatly admire once said that 'war is the ultimate failure of the imagination'; in that spirit, may the poets imagining and writing about peace bring us closer."

Kim Jensen (Baltimore, MD) lives with her husband, Palestinian painter Zahi Khamis, and their two children. Her novel about a turbulent love affair between a Palestinian exile and an American student is *The Woman I Left Behind*, (Curbstone Press, 2006). "Rock Bottom" is a selection from her *Bread Alone* (forthcoming, Syracuse Univ. Press) which explores the personal and collective despair engendered by the Bush era doctrine of endless war. "Paradoxically, this 'rock bottom' is also the place where we feel (viscerally), imagine (colorfully) and know (with certainty) the essential principals for building peace among people."

June Jordan (1936-2002) born in Harlem to Jamaican immigrants, has published twenty-seven books of poetry, political essay, and prose. A lifelong politically radical poet who emerged from the Black Arts movement, Jordan founded the Poetry for the People program at the University of California, Berkeley, was a regular columnist for *The Progressive*, and an active and outspoken participant in the peace movement and other liberationist movements since the 1950s.

Fady Joudah (Houston, TX) is a Palestinian American physician and was a field member of Doctors Without Borders in 2002 and 2005, in Zambia and Darfur respectively. His first poetry collection, *The Earth in the Attic* (2008) won the Yale Series for Younger Poets, and his translations of Mahmoud Darwish's recent poetry, *The Butterfly's Burden* (Copper Canyon Press, 2008) won the UK's society of authors award for Arabic translation (Saif Ghobash-Banipal award). "Peace universalizes and does not monopolize suffering."

Jennifer Karmin (Chicago, IL) has published poems in the anthologies *A Sing Economy* (Flim Forum Press, 2008) and *The City Visible: Chicago Poetry for the New Century* (Cracked Slab Books, 2007). "One of the jobs of the poet is to remind us of what's happening in the world and to help us think of these things in new ways. The work we make documents both resistance to war and paths to peace."

Diane Kendig (Lynn, MA) is working on a collection titled *The Places We Find Ourselves*. "My first book *A Tunnel of Flute Song* (1980) recalls the image of a flute, but does not place it in its original context of peace, as I am glad to finally do in this anthology."

Yusef Komunyakaa, born in 1947 to descendants from Trinidad, is the author of over a dozen books of poetry, including his prize-winning collection of Vietnam poems, *Dien Cai Dau* (Wesleyan, 1988) and the Pulitzer Prize winning *Neon Vernacular* (Wesleyan 1993). He served in the army during the Vietnam War as an information specialist and editor for the military paper, *Southern Cross*, covering major actions, interviewing fellow soldiers, and publishing articles on Vietnamese history and literature. In his words, "language is what can liberate or imprison the human psyche...we are responsible for our lives and the words we use."

Karen Kovacik (Indianapolis, IN) directs the creative writing program at IUPUI. Her most recent book is *Metropolis Burning* (Cleveland State, 2005). "I am grateful to be part of this project that offers images of peace."

Marilyn Krysl (Boulder, CO) has had fiction and poetry appear in the *Atlantic, The Nation, The New Republic, Best American Short Stories, O. Henry Prize Stories.* Her fourth story collection, *Dinner With Osama,* won Notre Dame's Richard Sullivan Prize in 2008. "I like William Stafford's remark that every war has two losers. I have extended it to read: every war has two losers and they assist each other in committing suicide. Also I aspire to Gandhi's declaration: 'I must become the change I wish to see in the world.'"

Tom Kryss (Charlestown, OH) is the author of *Downwind from the Fires of Nothingness* (Kirpan Press), *In a Time without Sunflowers* (Bottle of Smoke Press), *The Search for The Reason Why* (Bottom Dog Press 2007). "In the words of Mr. Rodney Glen King of Los Angeles, I continue to ask, 'Why can't we all just get along?'"

Gerry LaFemina (Frostburg, MD) is the author of the book of poems *The Parakeets of Brooklyn* (Bordighera Press, 2004). He is co-editor, with Chad Prevost, of *Evensong: Contemporary American Poets on Spirituality* (Bottom Dog Press 2007). He teaches at Frostburg State University where he directs the Frostburg Center for Creative Writing. "Poetry, for me, is a type of prayer. It requires attention of the writer and of the reader; it begs us to stop, to find the spark of the sublime in every word, in every image, and via the imagination, in the world around us."

Geoffrey A. Landis (Berea, OH) has a recent story "Still On the Road," featuring Jack Kerouac and Neal Cassady, in Isaac Asimov's *Science Fiction* magazine December, 2008. "About poetry and peace, about all I can say is that although poetry may be hard, from all the evidence, peace seems to be even harder."

Naton Leslie (Ballston Spa, NY) has a recent book of poetry in *Emma Saves Her Life* (Word Tech/Turning Point Books 2007). "Peace is as much a resource as it is a state of being and a goal. If we can find peace, we can use it to make other powerful things happen, like poetry."

Denise Levertov (1923-1997) was born in England and served as a civilian nurse in England during WW II. She lived in New York City and finally Seattle, WA. An outspoken voice against the Vietnam War, she joined The War Resister's League. Her book of prose ,*The Poet in the World* (1974) and her most recent book of poetry *The Life Around Us: Last Poems* (1997), are both from New Directions Publishing. "I don't think one can accurately measure the historical effectiveness of a poem; but one does know, of course, that books influence individuals; and individuals, although they are part of large economic and social processes, influence history. Every mass is after all made up of millions of individuals."

Lyn Lifshin (Vienna, VA) has a recent book in *Another Woman Who Looks Like Me* (Black Sparrow/ David Godine, 2006), selected for the Paterson Award for Literary Excellence and a finalist of the Paterson Poetry Prize.

Rachel Loden (Palo Alto, CA) Her book *Dick of the Dead* is forthcoming from Ahsahta Press. "I've always thought that Mayakovsky's 'cloud in trousers' was as good a way as any to describe poetry; peace, perhaps, is having the wherewithal to drift in and out of your trousers, and let them take you where they will."

Audre Lorde (1934-1992) began publishing in 1962. As a Black gay writer she has become a voice of resistance and tolerance. Two strong collections are *Chosen Poems: Old and New* (Norton,1982) and *A Burst of Light* (Firebrand, 1988). "I have come to believe over and over again that what is most important to me must be spoken, made verbal and shared, even at the risk of having it bruised or misunderstood."

Christina Lovin (Lancaster, KY) is the author of *Little Fires* (2008), #55 in the New Women's Voices Poetry Series from Finishing Line Press. "Poetry is a way of finding a small island of peace in an endless sea of turmoil and war: sometimes you don't realize you've found it until you're washed up, nearly drowned, on the shore and find that, if only for a few moments, you're saved."

Robert Lowell (1917-1977) was a conscientious objector during World War II and served time in jail for his refusal to serve, which he wrote about in "Memories of West Street and Lepke." Despite a lifelong bout with bipolar illness, Lowell was probably the most celebrated American poet of his time, an outspoken supporter of Civil Rights, and a lifelong critic of American empire. His participation in the 1967 March on the Pentagon is enshrined in Norman Mailer's *Armies of the Night*.

Dave Lucas (Cleveland, OH) is the recipient of a Henry Hoyns Fellowship at the University of Virginia and a 2005 Discovery/*The Nation* Prize; his poems have appeared in *The Paris Review, Poetry, Slate, The Threepenny Review*, and *The Virginia Quarterly Review*. He is a doctoral student in English at the University of Michigan.

Shara McCallum (Lewisburg, PA) has authored *Song of Thieves* (University of Pittsburg Press, 2003). "Nothing I could say is as relevant or beautiful as Yehuda Amichai's poem, 'Wildpeace.' Here are its closing lines: 'Let it come / like wildflowers, / suddenly, because the field / must have it: wildpeace.'"

Jack McGuane (Lakewood, OH) was designated Poet Laureate of Lakewood, 2006-2007; he is the author of a chapbook *Sleeping With My Socks* (deep cleveland press, 2008). He cites Abraham Maslow here: "A musician must make music, an artist must paint, a poet must write, if he is to be ultimately at peace with himself. What a man can be, he must be."

Katharyn Howd Machan (Ithaca, NY) is author of *The Professor Poems* (Main Street Rag Publishing Company, 2008). "I thank Herbert Gold for articulating many years ago that when people enter into the tragedy of war, they call upon doctors to heal physical wounds, but it is to poets they turn for the deeper healing needed."

Dora E. McQuaid (Taos, NM) is an award-winning poet, activist, speaker and teacher who combines her passion for language and performance with her dedication to activism. She lends art to activism internationally, both individually and with the all-female performance group she co-founded, The NeoSpinsters. Kate Bogle's short film, *One Woman's Voice*, (Penn State Media Sales) documents her activities.

Anna George Meek (Minneapolis, MN) has taught at The Loft Center and published in national magazines.

Edna St. Vincent Millay (1892-1950), poet and dramatist, was the first woman to receive the Pulitzer Prize in Poetry (1923) and the second woman to win the Frost Medal (1943), for her lifetime contribution to American poetry. Her play *Aria da Capo* was produced in Waldport,Oregon, at a Civilian Public Service Camp by conscientious objectors.

Robert Miltne, (Canton, OH) teaches at Kent State University Stark and in the Northeast Ohio MFA Creative Writing Consortium; his most recent collection is *Fellow Traveler* (Pudding House, 2006). "Peace is Pablo Neruda walking forth each day into the world, his poems under his arm like a loaf of bread, feeding justice to the hungry of the world."

Judith H. Montgomery (Bend, OR) has a recent book in *Pulse & Constellation* (Finishing Line Press, 2007). "May the words and poems in this anthology serve as threads for warp and weft, the weaving of the sacred and infinitely precious cloth of peace."

Liane Ellison Norman (Pittsburgh, PA) writes on nonviolence and civil liberties. Her first book of poetry, *The Duration of Grief,* was published in 2005 by Smoke & Mirrors Press. A book of her poetry and art by Ruey Brodine Morelli, entitled *Keep*, will be published fall of 2008 by Smoke & Mirrors Press. A biography, *Hammer of Justice: Molly Rush and the Plowshares Eight* was published in 1990 by PPI Books. She founded the Pittsburgh Peace Institute in 1984 to teach non-violent ways of conducting conflict. "I believe that people can conduct even very serious conflict with minimal or no violence."

Naomi Shihab Nye (born 1952) is a poet, songwriter and novelist, born to a Palestinian father and an American mother. The author and/or editor of more than 20 volumes, her books of poetry include *19 Varieties of Gazelle: Poems of the Middle East* (Greenwillow, 2002). In her open letter, "To Any Would-Be Terrorists," Nye writes: "Poetry humanizes us in a way that news, or even religion, has a harder time doing. A great Arab scholar, Dr. Salma Jayyusi, said, 'If we read one another, we won't kill one another.'"

Eric Pankey (Fairfax, VA) is the author of eight collections of poetry, the most recent of which is *The Pear as One Example: New and Selected Poems 1984-2008* (Ausable Press, 2008).

Kenneth Patchen (1911-1972) was born into an Ohio working-class family and became both a rebel poet and artist in Greenwich Village and San Francisco. His anti-novel *The Journal of Albion Moonlight* (1941) remains one of the strongest anti-war statements in American literature. "The best hope is that one of these days the ground will get disgusted enough just to walk away—leaving people with nothing more to stand on than what they have so bloody well stood for up to now."

Edwina Pendarvis (Huntington, WV) has taught at Marshall University since 1979. Her new collection of memoirs, *Raft Tide and Railroad: How We Lived and Died*, is forthcoming from Blair Mountain Press. "Wonder at the variety and beauty of life is essential to peace. And I don't know any work showing a greater sense of the mystery of the natural world, including humans as part of nature, than Charles Darwin's *The Origin of Species*, which concludes, 'From so simple a beginning, endless forms most beautiful and most wonderful have been, and are being evolved.'"

Robert Pinsky (born 1940) is the author of numerous books of poetry and prose, most recently *Gulf Music* (Farrar, Straus, Giroux, 2008), and he served as the Poet Laureate of the United States from 1997-2000. During his laureateship, he founded the Favorite Poem Project, extending the democracy of poetry and the poetry of democracy. In early 2003, Pinsky joined other poets in refusing to attend the White House event, "Poetry and the American Voice," in protest of the imminent war in Iraq.

Susan Azar Porterfield (DeKalb, IL) has two books of poetry including *In the Garden of Our Spines* (Mayapple Press, 2004) and *Beirut Redux* (Finishing Line Press, 2008). "I heard once that immediately after 9/11 people turned to reading poetry in great numbers."

Chad Prevost (Chattanooga, TN) is the author of *A Walking Cliche Coins a Phrase: Prose Poems and Microfictions* (Plain View Press 2008). "Although poetry will never stop war it does serve—among other things—as a signpost against forgetting and as a conscience for the better selves we can be."

Maj Ragain (Kent, OH) teaches at Kent State University and hosts open poetry readings, currently at the North Water Street Gallery. His most recent book of poems is *A Hungry Ghost Surrenders His Tackle Box* (Pavement Saw Press 2007). "The poem is a geode. Break it open. The kingdom is within."

Kenneth Rexroth (1905-1982), poet, translator, critic, was an outspoken poet of the Left and a strong advocate of peace. In his years in San Francisco he was a large influence on radical writing including Sam Hamill, Lawrence Ferlinghetti, and others. His *Complete Poems* is available from *Copper Canyon Press* (2003). "I write for one and only one purpose, to overcome the invincible ignorance of the traduced heart. My poems are acts of force and violence directed against the evil which murders us all."

Marilynn Rashid (Ferndale, MI) teaches Spanish at Wayne State University in Detroit. Recent poems and translations have appeared in *Absinthe*, *Marlboro Review*, and *Runes*. "William Stafford said, 'War prunes the tree—taking the best branches.' Poetry alone will not bring peace, but it helps us to see that tree, to honor it in its entirety, to at least imagine a way that it can flourish."

Adrienne Rich (born 1929) has been a leader in the women's liberation and gay liberation movements, galvanized by her celebrated poetry and essays. When *Diving Into the Wreck* received the National Book Award for Poetry, she accepted the award accompanied by Alice Walker and Audre Lorde on behalf of silenced women. In 1997, Rich refused the National Medal of Arts, stating that "I could not accept such an award from President Clinton or this White House because the very meaning of art, as I understand it, is incompatible with the cynical politics of this administration." In her words, "[art] means nothing if it simply decorates the dinner table of the power which holds it hostage."

Susan Rich (Seattle, WA) is the author of *The Cartographer's Tongue: Poems of the World and Cures Include Travel* (White Pine Press, 2000). Her third collection, *The Alchemist's Kitchen* is forthcoming from White Pine Press. "Art and virtue are measured in tiny grains" —Lu Chi's *Wen Fu*.

Rosaly DeMaios Roffman (Indiana, PA) teaches creative writing, Myth and literature. She co-edited *Life on the Line: Selections on Words and Healing* and is the author of *Going to Bed Whole* and *In the Fall of a Sparrow*. The recipient of a National Endowment Award and a Witter Bynner Foundation Grant for "ladino" poetry. "As poet and constant student of myth, I am at a loss to try to address that sense of urgency that seems to pervade the now—but if poetry energy can do anything—I wish it to address this world in crisis and to remind us of love and preservation with greater amplification—if not, let us document any evidence of what is recognizably human and miraculous, as we weep over and over at evidence of the unspeakable in the arena."

Lisa Rosen (Eugene OR) has a chapbook of poetry in *Bright Omens* (Traprock Press). "May we all be blessed to experience and share sweet peace."

Joseph Ross (Silver Spring, MD) is one of the early members of D.C. Poets Against the War. He co-edited *Cut Loose the Body: An Anthology of Poems on Torture and Fernando Botero's Abu Ghraib*. His poetry appears in many anthologies and journals, including *Poet Lore, Sojourners, Potomac,* and *Poetic Voices Without Borders*. "We can only create what we have first imagined."

Muriel Rukeyser (1913-1980) was a long standing political activist for women, the working class, and against war, her poems can be found in *The Collected Poems* (Univ. of Pittsburgh 2005). Her views on poetry and society are in her *The Life of Poetry* (Paris Press 1949). "However confused the scene of our life appears, however torn we may be who now do face that scene, it can be faced, and we can go on to be whole."

Lauren Rusk (Palo Alto, CA) is the author of a recent collection of poems : *Pictures in the Firestorm* (Plain View Press, 2007). "Contemplative reading and writing are acts of love; the more we encourage them, the more, I have reason to believe, we strengthen peace."

Michael Salinger (Mentor, OH) is poet, performer, director and playwright involved in promoting creative writing through performance and education. He is the co-author of *Outspoken!* (Heinemann) which teaches writing and speaking skills using poetry performance in the classroom. His *Well Defined— Vocabulary in Rhyme* is forthcoming from Boyd's Mills Press. "Most if not all confrontation arises from some sort of miscommunication. If people learn to appreciate poetry, maybe they can learn to appreciate nuance in language amidst the sound blurb bombardment from the powers who count on our not paying close attention."

Ed Sanders (Woodstock, NY) publishes the *Woodstock Journal* with his wife of over 36 years, the writer and painter Miriam R. Sanders. His years of war resistance extend from to the 1960's when he performed with The Fugs rock group into today with his most recent work the three volume *America: A History in Verse*. His most recent title is: *Poems for New Orleans* (North Atlantic Books 2008). "So, in the midst of our struggle we need to slow down, and tend to our garden."

Sappho (625-570 B.C.) has been called "the greatest female poet of antiquity." A great promulgator of the lyric poetic tradition, Sappho's poetry turned away from the Homeric epic and toward the personal and the erotic for its inspiration. Few of Sappho's poems from her nine books survive, most only in fragmented form.

Joanne Seltzer (Schenectady, NY) is the author of the poetry collection *Women Born During Tornadoes* (Plain View Press 2008). She sees the poem "Making Peace in Jerusalem" as a metaphor for the Israeli-Palestinian conflict: "Jews and Arabs, uncomfortable cousins, must find a way to broker peace because no acceptable alternative exists....As poets substitute emotion for meaning, we savage illusions based on denial and goad philosophers into calling us liars."

Mike Schneider (Pittsburgh, PA) has poems in many journals, including *5 AM, Shenandoah*, and *Poetry*, and a chapbook, *Rooster* (Main Street Rag, 2004). He organized the February 2003 reading in Pittsburgh's Market Square at which 27 poets in 15-degree cold and light snow expressed their opposition to then impending war in Iraq.

Aharon Shabtai (born 1939) is a leading Israeli poet and translator, having published over fifteen books of poetry and translation, including the blistering *J'Accuse* (2003). In 2006, he refused to participate in the Eizenberg Shalom International Poetry Festival in Jerusalem, writing that he opposed "an international poetry festival in a city in which the Arab inhabitants are oppressed systematically and cruelly imprisoned between walls, deprived of their rights and living spaces, humiliated in checkpoints....I think that even poets were not allowed in the past, and not in the present, to ignore persecutions and discriminations on a racial or national basis."

Karl Shapiro (1913-2000) served in the army during World War II, and won the Pulitzer Prize for his book of poems, *V-Letter and Other Poems* (Reynal & Hitchcock, 1944), written while overseas. His subsequent book, published while the Poetry Consultant for the Library of Congress, *Trial of a Poet and Other Poems* (Reynal & Hitchcock, 1947), explores the aftermath of military victory and the dark moral consequences of the nuclear age.

Jeanne Shannon (Albuquerque, NM) is editor/publisher of The Wildflower Press in Albuquerque, New Mexico. *Angelus*, a collection of her poetry, was published in 2006 by Fithian Press. "For me, poetry, especially poetry that celebrates the natural world, is a path to inner peace, and those who have inner peace are not likely to make war."

Derek Sheffield (Leavenworth, WA) has a recent collection in *A Revised Account of the West* (*Flyway*/Iowa State University, 2008). "We can help end war by encouraging a more stringent biologic education worldwide, so that every individual of our species is aware that our species is only one of millions, so that each of us can imagine the billions of evolutions that have led to *now* and *here*, so that at least once a day we lose ourselves to wonder."

Deema K. Shehabi (Pleasant Hill, CA) is a Palestinian poet who grew up in the Arab world. Her poems have appeared widely in anthologies and journals such as The *Kenyon Review, Drunken Boat,* and *The Poetry of Arab Women.* She is currently Vice-President of the RAWI (Radius of Arab-American Writers). "The 'ghazal' was written out of my strong-rooted desire to formally lament the ongoing state of affairs in the West Bank and Gaza. In particular, those tragic occurrences, juxtaposed against a personal, sometimes discursive narrative, gave the poem its impetus. The rhyme and refrain inherent to the structure of the ghazal proved grounding to the leaping imagination."

Vivian Shipley (North Haven, CT) is the editor of *Connecticut Review* from Southern Connecticut State University. Her seventh book of poems, *Hardboot: Poems New & Old* (Southeastern Louisiana University Press, 2005) won the Paterson Award for Sustained Literary Achievement. "Evil in this world will not be tamed, widespread injustice will not be curbed but poets can offer poems as prayers for peace, bear witness and write to record the struggle of the heart, the mind, the body ensnared by powers that cannot be understood or controlled."

Enid Shomer is the author of four collections of poetry and two collections of short fiction. Her most recent book, *Tourist Season: Stories* (Random House, 2007), was selected for Barnes & Noble's "Discover Great New Writers" program and also won the Gold Medal in Fiction from the State of Florida.

Martha Silano (Seattle, WA) is the author of *Blue Positive* (Steel Toe Books). "I vote for the Native American 'coup' stick: with it a warrior snuck up on his enemy, tapped him on the back, and in this way earned more honor and respect than if he had actually killed him."

David Sklar ranges from poetry in *Wormwood Review* to political satire in *The FarceHaven Tribune.* His novella is *Shadow of the Antlered Bird* (Drollerie Press). "My work deals with human recklessness and the consequences of our actions on the world around and the world within."

Gary Snyder (born 1930) grew up in the Pacific Northwest, and has proven himself as poet, translator, essayist and lecturer. His book of poems *Turtle Island* (New Directions, 1975) won the Pulitzer Prize. Among his books of essays is the essential *The Practice of the Wild* (North Point Press, 1990) and most recent *Back on the Fire* (Counterpoint Press, 2005). "Find your place on the planet. Dig in, and take responsibility from there."

William Stafford (1914-1993) was born in Hutchinson, KS, and served four years as a conscientious objector in Civilian Public Service camps during World War II, which he writes about in his memoir, *Down in My Heart* (1947). He won the National Book Award for his first book, *Traveling Through the Dark* (1962). A lifelong pacifist, and one of pacifism's most thoughtful proponents (evident in *Every War Has Two Losers: William Stafford on Peace and War*), Stafford wrote every morning at dawn, in his words, to do "maintenance work on my integrity."

Andrew Sydlik (Pittsburgh, PA) "I think of both poetry and peace as ways to re-imagine the world I live in."

Wislawa Szymborska (born 1923) is a Polish poet and essayist. Her witty poems, written in everyday language, poignantly and sometimes acidly detail the complexities of the human condition. She won the Nobel Prize in Literature in 1996.

Rosemary Wahtola Trommer (Placerville, CO) is an organic fruit grower and lives on the Gunnison and San Miguel Rivers in southwest Colorado. Her most recent collection of poems is *Four Corners: The Intimate Landscape* (Durango Herald Small Press, 2008). "My poem-a-day practice helps me to make peace with what is, moment by moment."

Joanna Trzeciak (Cleveland, OH) teaches in the Translation Studies Program at Kent State University and creative writing in the NEO MFA program. Her translations have appeared in *The New Yorker, The New York Times, Atlantic Monthly, Harper's*. Her *Miracle Fair: Selected Poems of Wislawa Szymborska* was awarded the Heldt Translation Prize. *Alarm Clock: Selected Poems of Tadeusz Rozewicz* is forthcoming from W.W. Norton.

Chase Twichell (Keene, NY) is the author of six books of poetry. *Horses Where the Answers Should Have Been: New & Selected Poems* is forthcoming from Copper Canyon in 2009. She is Editor of Ausable Press. "Architecture" is from *The Snow Watcher* (Ontario Review Press, 1998). "The human mind makes war, peace, and art. A poem can penetrate chaos and camouflage and remind us that this is our one and only world and our one and only life."

Jon Volkmer (Collegeville, PA) is director of creative writing at Ursinus College in Collegeville, Pennsylvania. He is the author of the poetry collection, *The Art of Country Grain Elevators* (Bottom Dog Press 2005) and the travel memoir *Eating Europe*.

Michael Waters (Ocean, NJ) is the author of *Darling Vulgarity* (BOA Editions 2006). As Nazi Hermann Goering said at Nuremberg, "The people can always be brought to the bidding of their leaders. That is easy. All you have to do is tell them they are being attacked and denounce the peacemakers for lack of patriotism and exposing the country to danger. It works the same in any country."

Mary E. Weems (Cleveland, OH) is the author of *An Unmistakable Shade of Red and the Obama Chronicles* (Bottom Dog Press, 2008). "I believe in life and in living in peace with all people. War is the opposite of peace—I'm against war for any reason. Conflict should always be resolved in non-violent ways decided upon by the two or more sides."

Thomas A. West, Jr. (Morrison, CO) has recent poems appearing in *California Quarterly* and *The Wisconsin Review*. "Ice does not suffice! The warmth of life and living, of digging in between and beyond what is 'real,' of 'licking honey off a thorn'—all that is closer to poetry, I think."

Walt Whitman (1819-1892) was born in Long Island, NY, into a Quaker family. With *Leaves of Grass*, first published in 1855, Whitman established himself as one of the great poets not only of American literature, but of world literature. His great poem, "Song of Myself," and his Civil War poems—partly based on his experience nursing wounded Union soldiers in field hospitals—demonstrate his great compassion, his imaginative empathy, and his longing for human union.

Steve Wilson (San Marcos, TX) has recent work in such journals as *New American Writing, Beloit Poetry Journal,* and The *North American Review*. "The purpose of poetry today has to be that it asks us to stop and think, to consider, to examine and examine again."

Sarah Zale (Port Townsend, WA) teaches writing at Edmonds Community College and the University of Phoenix in the Pacific Northwest. She has published poetry, a biography, non-fiction articles and short stories. She is the former Editor-in-Chief of *Pitkin Review,* a literary journal at Goddard College. In 2006 she visited Israel and Palestine on a peace delegation with the Compassionate Listening Project. "It is the poet in all of us that will save us."

The Editors

Larry Smith is founder/director of Bottom Dog Press since 1985. He is the author of 8 books of poetry, a book of memoirs, *Milldust and Roses* (Ridgeway 2002), three books of fiction, including *Faces and Voices: Tales* (Bird Dog Publishing, 2006), and literary biographies on Kenneth Patchen and Lawrence Ferlinghetti. He has edited the following books for Bottom Dog Press: *Cleveland Poetry Scenes: A Panorama and Anthology* (2008), *d.a.levy and the mimeograph revolution* (2007); *Family Matters: Poems of Our Families* (2005); *America Zen: A Gathering of Poets* (2004), and *Working Hard for the Money: America's Working Poor* with Mary Weems. He is professor emeritus of Bowling Green State University, Firelands College.

Ann Smith lives in Huron, Ohio, with her husband Larry. She is a professor emerita from the University of Toledo Health Sciences Center. She is a Clinical Nurse Specialist in Adult Mental Health Nursing and provides counseling, Therapeutic Touch, and Reiki at her Reiki and Counseling Center in Sandusky, Ohio. Ann was co-editor of *Family Matters: Poems of Our Families* (2005) and has written articles on family relationships in those families experiencing chronic pain. Ann and Larry are founding members of Voices for Peace and Justice and Converging Paths: Sandusky Bay Meditation Center in Northern Ohio. She instructs in mediation and non-violent communication.

Philip Metres lives in University Heights, Ohio, and is the author of *To See the Earth* (poetry, 2008), *Behind the Lines: War Resistance Poetry on the American Homefront since 1941* (criticism, 2007), *Catalogue of Comedic Novelties: Selected Poems of Lev Rubinstein* (2004), and *A Kindred Orphanhood: Selected Poems of Sergey Gandlevsky* (2003), and two chapbooks. He has been involved in the peace movement since the 1980s; he co-founded the Bloomington Coalition for Peace (Bloomington, Indiana) in the 1990s, and has worked with Pax Christi, Committee for Peace in the Middle East, Peace Action, and Tikkun. He is an associate professor of English at John Carroll University in Cleveland, Ohio. His paternal grandparents hail from Lebanon; were it not for Ellis Island, his last name would be Abourjaili. See his webpage concerning peace and poetry: <behindthelinespoetry.blogspot.com>

Acknowledgments

We thank the following authors and publications for the right to reprint the following copyrighted material.

"Twigs" (parts 115 and 117) **Taha Muhammad Ali**, translated by Peter Cole, from *So What: New & Selected Poems 1971-2005.* © 2006 by Taha Muhammad Ali. English translation © 2000, 2006 by Peter Cole. Reprinted with the permission of Copper Canyon Press, <www.coppercanyonpress.org>.

"Wild Peace" by **Yehuda Amichai** from *The Selected Poetry of Yehuda Amichai, Newly Revised and Expanded edition,* © 1996 by The University of California Press.

"Pray for Peace" by **Ellen Bass** from *The Human Line.* © 2007 by Ellen Bass. Reprinted with the permission of Copper Canyon Press, <www.coppercanyon press.org>.

"Prayer for Picket Line" and "Prayer for the Morning Headlines" by **Daniel Berrigan**, from *And the Risen Bread: Selected Poems,* © 1998 Fordham University Press.

"Call and Answer" by **Robert Bly**, from *My Sentence Was a Thousand Years of Joy* © 2005. HarperCollins, by permission of the author.

"We Need a War" by **Mark Brazaitis** originally appeared in *Poetry East.*

"If a Boddhisatva" by **David Budbill** from *While We've Still Got Feet.* © 2005 by David Budbill. Reprinted with the permission of Copper Canyon Press, <www.coppercanyonpress.org>.

"Waiting for the Barbarians" from **C. P. Cavafy**: *Collected Poems,* translated by Edmund Keeley and Philip Sherrard, © 1975, 1992 by Edmund Keeley and Philip Sherrard; reproduced with the permission of Princeton University Press.

"Savoring The World" by **Dane Cervine** appeared in *The Jeweled Net of Indra* (Plain View Press 2007).

"Dandelions" by **Hayan Charara** first appeared in *Heartlands Today* (Vol 4, 1994), and it was reprinted in his *The Alchemist's Diary* (Hanging Loose Press, 2001).

"For No More Reason" by **Robert Creeley**, from *Selected Poems: 1945-2005* © 2005, The University of California Press.

"Reincarnation of the Peace Sign" by **Jim Daniels** originally appeared in the literary journal, *Chautauqua.* His "Something Like a Sonnet for Something Like Peace" originally appeared in the literary journal, *Poetry in Performance.*

"State of Siege" (parts 171 and 173), by **Mahmoud Darwish**, translated by Fady Joudah, from *The Butterfly's Burden.* © 2007 by Mahmoud Darwish. Translation © 2007 by Fady Joudah. Reprinted with the permission of Copper Canyon Press, <www.coppercanyon press.org>.

"On the Way Home" is "Revolutionary Letter #81" in **Diane di Prima's** *Revolutionary Letters* (Enlarged edition, Last Gasp Press, 2007).

"The Federal Building," reprinted from *Arab on Radar* by **Angele Ellis** (Six Gallery Press, 2007). © Copyright Angele Ellis.

Other Books from Bottom Dog Press

Cleveland Poetry Scenes: A Panorama and Anthology
eds. Nina Gibans, Mary Weems, Larry Smith
978-1933964-17-1   304 pgs. $20

America Zen: A Gathering of Poets
eds. Ray McNiece and Larry Smith
0-933087-91-8   224 pgs. $15.00

Evensong: Contemporary American Poets on Spirituality
eds. Gerry LaFemina & Chad Prevost
1-933964-01-4   276 pgs. $18

Family Matters: Poems of Our Families
eds. Ann Smith and Larry Smith
0-933087-95-0   230 pgs. $16.00

Bar Stories, edited by Nan Byrne
14 stories set in the bars of America
978-1-933964-09-6   176 pgs. $14.00

d.a.levy & the mimeograph revolution
eds. Ingrid Swanberg & Larry Smith
1-933964-07-3   276 pgs. & dvd $25

Our Way of Life: Poems
by Ray McNiece
978-1-933964-14-0 128 pgs. $14.00

The Search for the Reason Why:
New and Selected Poems by Tom Kryss
0-933087-96-9 192 pgs. $14.00

Hunger Artist: Childhood in the Suburbs
by Joanne Jacobson
978-1-933964-11-9   132 pgs. $16
http://smithdocs.net